When Faith
Becomes Sight

HEAVEN

JENNIFER ROTHSCHILD

Lifeway Press®
Brentwood, Tennessee

Published by Lifeway Press® • © 2025 Jennifer Rothschild

ISBN: 978-1-4300-9034-2 • Item: 005846960
Dewey decimal classification: 236.24
Subject headings: Heaven \ FUTURE LIFE \ PARADISE

To order additional copies of this resource, write to Lifeway Resources Customer Service; 200 Powell Place, Suite 100, Brentwood, TN, 37027-7707; order online at lifeway.com; fax 615.251.5933; phone toll free 800.458.2772; or email orderentry@lifeway.com.

Printed in the United States of America

Lifeway Women Bible Studies
Lifeway Resources
200 Powell Place, Suite 100,
Brentwood, TN, 37027-7707

Cover design by Lauren Ervin

EDITORIAL TEAM, LIFEWAY WOMEN BIBLE STUDIES

Becky Loyd
Director, Lifeway Women

Tina Boesch
Manager

Chelsea Waack
Production Leader

Mike Wakefield
Content Editor

Tessa Morrell
Production Editor

Lauren Ervin
Art Director

Sarah Hobbs
Graphic Designer

Table of Contents

About the Author

Heaven: When Faith Becomes Sight is Jennifer's ninth video-based Bible study with Lifeway. It follows her popular Bible studies, *Amos: An Invitation to the Good Life*; *Take Courage: A Study of Haggai*; *Psalm 23: The Shepherd With Me*; *Hosea: Unfailing Love Changes Everything*; and *Me, Myself, and Lies: A Thought-Closet Makeover*, among others.

Jennifer has shared her inspiring messages to audiences across the country and through media outlets including: *The Dr. Phil Show*, *Good Morning America*, *The Today Show*, and *The Billy Graham Television Special*. She's the featured teacher and founder of Fresh Grounded Faith women's events and hosts the *4:13 Podcast* where she offers practical encouragement and biblical wisdom to help women live the "I can" life. Jennifer is also the publisher of the popular online leadership library called womensministry.net.

Jennifer is known for her substance, signature wit, and down-to-earth style. A unique mix of profound and playful, she weaves biblical truth with relatable stories, making God's Word accessible to those just starting out in Scripture and endearing to those who have walked with Christ for years.

She's a C. S. Lewis junkie, an obsessive audiobook listener, a dark chocolate lover, and she drinks way too much strong coffee.

She's been blind since age fifteen and says the greatest lesson she's learned in the dark is that it doesn't have to be well with your circumstances to be well with your soul. Jennifer is a boy mom and a GiGi of four (and counting) who lives in Missouri with her husband, whom she affectionately calls her very own Dr. Phil!

Connect with Jennifer at **jenniferrothschild.com/heaven**.

Four Things You Need to Know Before Starting This Study

(OKAY, FIVE; YOU'LL SEE)

1 YOU HAVE FREE ACCESS TO SEVEN VIDEO TEACHINGS ON PAGE 225

Here's the way to best use the videos: First, read page 8, "When You Smell the Flowers." This is my note to you, so don't skip it. I wrote it to you!

Then, gather with your group and watch the Session One video titled, "Getting the Scoop on Heaven" and take notes on page 10. You can do this study solo, but we believe it is best experienced in a group setting. So, join with your people at church, or pull some neighbors together, or just gather some friends and Bible study buddies to study with! You need them. They need you. God's Word is sweet when we share it together.

After watching the Session One video, begin your personal study in Session One: "Your Father's House" (p. 12).

Each week of study includes four days of personal study and concludes with a summary of *Takeaway Truths* and a fifth day titled *Dash Living Day*.

2 YOU WILL ENJOY DASH LIVING DAYS

The main goal of the *Heaven* Bible study is for us to gain a biblical understanding of Heaven so we can live faithfully in the now with eager anticipation of our future.

But also, this completed Bible study will become a practical resource for you and the people you love.

Every fifth day of each week of study will be a *Dash Living Day*. Often on a tombstone or in a news article about someone who has died, a birth date and death date are presented with a dash in between. For example, C. S. Lewis (11/29/1898–11/22/1963) is my favorite dead author. The dash between those dates represents what happened to that person between the date of birth and the date of death. At this moment, we are all living in the dashes. And how we live now and what we record about our lives becomes the legacy that outlives us.

So, *Dash Living Days* give us a chance to reflect and record important things about how we best live our lives in this moment and what we want others to know when we're gone. (You may want to make your loved ones aware these words exist and how to locate them.)

3 YOU WILL WATCH A VIDEO TEACHING FOLLOWING EACH WEEK OF PERSONAL STUDY

Each week of personal study is followed by a video teaching that provides insight and reinforces what you learned in your personal study. (To access the video teaching sessions, use the instructions in the back of your Bible study book.)

4 YOU HAVE EXTRA RESOURCES ONLINE AND LEADER HELP ON PAGE 210

If you're leading a group, you'll find Leader Helps on page 210 and other free resources at **lifeway.com/heaven**. You can also get tons of extra resources to enhance group and personal study at **jenniferrothschild.com/heaven**. Go there to get ideas, a *Heaven* playlist, video message summaries, and more.

5 YOU ARE LOVED

I love and appreciate you and am so thankful you care about studying Heaven. And just to show you how much I appreciate you reading this page all the way down to number five, scan this QR code for a special *Heaven* gift from me to you!

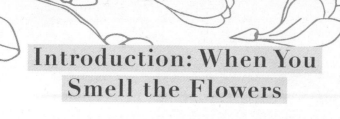

Introduction: When You Smell the Flowers

"I have come home at last! This is my real country! I belong here.
This is the land I have been looking for all my life . . . "[1]

C. S. LEWIS

I've walked many miles in the dark, thus my eyes are drawn to the place where there is no more night, no darkness at all. Since becoming blind at age fifteen, I've held the arms of friends, family, and strangers to navigate the unending darkness. I've held tight to my faith and been held by God's grace through every dark day. And I've also held a white cane. I have definitely walked by faith and not by sight—in a very literal sense.

I'll never forget how Mike, my mobility instructor, finished up my first lesson of learning to walk in the dark. I was seventeen years old when I got my first white cane, and with it I got Mike, the amazing guy who taught me how to use it. During that first lesson, he showed me how to navigate safely and helped me gain some independence. He walked me around my neighborhood, pointing out how to hold the cane, how to tap it, and how to anticipate all the rough places I would encounter.

Sweaty from the Miami heat and probably from the stress I felt, we turned the last corner toward my home. He paused and asked, "Do you smell it?"

I stopped and breathed in my surroundings. I did smell it. A lush bush of blooming hibiscus was right there on the corner near my home.

"When you smell the flowers," Mike said, "you know you're almost home."

So, my friend, I ask you what Mike asked me, "Do you smell it?"

Pause and breathe in your surroundings.

The fragrance of Heaven is wafting along the path you walk even if you haven't noticed it yet.

It is your reminder that home, your Father's house, is just around the corner—one breath, one heartbeat away. Even if Heaven came way too soon for someone you love or if you think (and hope) it is decades away for you, it is still our eternal home. By faith, it is our unseen reality that makes all we see here beam with real, unshakeable hope.

On this side of eternity, we each walk by faith, not by sight.

But there will be a day when the fragrance of those flowers is so strong that we will know, we will know we are almost home. Yet that scent of eternity is drawing us even now to the beauty, the hope, and the assurance of our ultimate home: Heaven.

So, as we navigate through bright and dark days here, we hold on to our faith, each other, and we are held by God's grace. The shadows we face and feel here—sickness, uncertainty, stress, sorrow—will all eventually lift when we are captivated by that sweet aroma that ushers us into the presence of the One whose face we will clearly see!

Over the next seven weeks together, we will gain a biblical understanding of Heaven. As we discover what the Bible says about our glorious unending, we will be fortified in the face of uncertainty, anchored in deep spiritual serenity, and grounded in eternity.

So, let's keep pressing on until that day when our faith becomes sight!

I'm so grateful we're learning this together. Onward and upward!

Love,

Jennifer

INTRODUCTION: GETTING THE SCOOP ON HEAVEN

BEFORE THE VIDEO

Welcome and Prayer

WATCH THE VIDEO

Death is not the end of our ___stories___. Death is simply the ___comma___ that separates us and transitions us into that forever story of our life.

What we ___think___ and what we ___know___ about Heaven will determine how we ___live___.

Heaven is a literal ___place___ where God dwells, where born again believers in Christ go when they ___die___ or when Christ ___returns___, whichever comes first.

Blue flowers in literature, especially in German romantic literature represent ___transcendant___ longing, and an ___aching___ for the eternal.

The ___Bible___ is what expands and illuminates our ___vision___ and our ___view___ of Heaven.

Go to **jenniferrothschild.com/heaven** to get an email summary of this video teaching in your inbox. Plus, check out my *Heaven* playlist to encourage you as you live what you learn.

To access the video teaching sessions, use the instructions in the back of your Bible study book.

CONVERSATION GUIDE

- What's the first thing you think of when you hear the word Heaven?

- If someone asked you what you thought Heaven was going to be like, what would you say?

- What has shaped your view of Heaven? What has been the strongest influence on your view?

- Does your view of Heaven affect how you live? If so, how? If not, why should it?

- What's one point/story/truth from the video teaching that resonated with you? Why?

- What are you hoping to get out of this study on Heaven?

SESSION ONE

"Do not let your hearts be troubled. You believe in God; believe also in me. My Father's house has many rooms; if that were not so, would I have told you that I am going there to prepare a place for you? And if I go and prepare a place for you, I will come back and take you to be with me that you also may be where I am."

JOHN 14:1-3

YOUR FATHER'S HOUSE

Heaven is often misrepresented, misunderstood, and perhaps missed altogether because of a lack of clarity about what it is and who goes there.

This week, you will get a working understanding of how Scripture speaks of Heaven and experience the comfort and confidence that knowledge provides. First, we'll examine how Heaven is spoken of from creation to the cross, especially how the Old Testament talks about the afterlife. Second, we'll examine how Heaven is referred to from the resurrection to the return of Christ, looking at how New Testament writers talked about what happens and where we go if we die before Christ returns. And third, we'll deal with how the Bible talks of Heaven after Christ's return, noting where we will spend all of eternity.

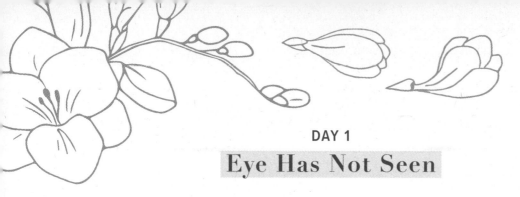

DAY 1

Eye Has Not Seen

"Earth's crammed with Heaven, and every common bush afire with God:
But only he who sees takes off his shoes."[1]

ELIZABETH BARRETT BROWNING

Heaven. It's your glorious unending. Your forever home. The place your faith becomes sight. I'm so grateful we're spending the next six weeks in Heaven together! (Grin!) So settle in, take a deep breath, and let's start. (You'll notice at the beginning of each day I've written a prayer based on the Scripture in parentheses. Let these prayers prepare your heart for each day of study.)

*Lord, guide us through Your Spirit to know truth
and understand Your holy Word. Amen (John 16:13).*

As I write this, I'm standing at my glass-top desk, feeling the warmth of sunlight bathe the room.

Sometimes I stand here in my office and sense the soft afternoon light seeping through the window. Though I can't see it, I know it's there, and I lift my eyes and imagine what lies beyond the pane. In my mind's eye I see the carpet of grass and the unruly limbs of the lazy oak that often scrape my window frame on a windy day. But then I imagine beyond; I see the blue flowers.

Full disclosure: there are no blue flowers outside my window, but I'm looking way beyond my front yard. I'm casting my imaginative gaze to a faraway place where I dream blue flowers grow.

You see, the blue flower in literature represents longing. It was a central symbol of the Romanticism movement, portraying a desire, yearning, and love of the eternal.[2] And oh, how I ache for the eternal. C. S. Lewis called himself, "a votary of the Blue Flower."[3]

But here's the thing: my physical eyes can't see a blue flower. A degenerative retinal disease caused me to lose my eyesight when I was fifteen, so I have lived in physical darkness longer than I ever lived in physical light. And quite honestly, I don't even have a good visual memory of a blue flower. But my fingertips have brushed the delicate petals of a blue hydrangea. I have breathed in its sweet, subtle fragrance. This has awakened in me a beautiful longing for that which I can't even see.

It awakens what no eye has seen—images of Heaven, the place where I hope blue flowers grow.

> Is there anything in your life that awakens an awareness of the eternal or a desire for Heaven? If so, describe it.

It's interesting that often what we see or feel *here* awakens in us a longing, a desire for *there*, for Heaven. Even the temporary pulses with the echo of the eternal. Even the tangible can quicken our heartbeat and cast our gaze toward the transcendent. Yet what our hearts long for, no eye has ever seen.

Could that be what Paul was talking about in 1 Corinthians 2:9?

Let's see.

Read the verse and list the main points.

No one has seen, heard or understood what God has done for everyone who love Him.

Now, go back and read the verses surrounding verse 9. How do they help you understand what it means?

I've always thought this verse was talking about Heaven. I've even heard sermons where the preacher used that verse to explain how beyond our imagination Heaven must be. Yet when we read verse 9 in context, we see Paul was using Old Testament passages (Isa. 52:15; 64:4) to explain that now, through the Holy Spirit, believers can see with enlightened eyes God's wisdom in Christ. Only eyes opened by the power of the Holy Spirit can see such beautiful mystery.

So, spoiler alert. Verse 9 is not talking about Heaven. It's referring to the gospel.

Finding out that verse isn't about Heaven might be a little alarming, especially if, like me, you thought it was. But don't you just love learning how deep and beautiful its actual meaning is? And isn't it exciting to find out we have so much to learn, and maybe unlearn, about Heaven?

Can we apply the "no eye has seen . . . [what] God has prepared" idea of that verse to the mystery of Heaven? And can we let it be the fragrance of a blue flower awakening our longing for eternity? Maybe so, if we listen to the One who has actually seen what our eyes have not.

Find John 3:13 and John 14:2–3. Write all three verses in order below and then read them aloud as one seamless paragraph a few times.

No one has ever gone into Heaven except the one who came from Heaven – the Son of Man.
In My Father's house there are many rooms; if it were not so, I would have told you. I'm going there to prepare a place for you.

Did you hear that? Jesus came from Heaven and has exclusive expert authority on Heaven. He called that place, "My Father's house" (John 14:2). His eye had literally seen it, so we can trust what He says about what our eye has not seen.

> Pause here and ponder why Jesus may have chosen to call Heaven our Father's house. What implications flow from that title? What emotions and thoughts do you have about it?

I call my earthly father "Hero Dad" because he was. Though I lived thousands of miles away, knowing my dad was home in his house in Florida brought me such a sense of security. I knew I always had a place in my father's house. Even as a married woman, knowing he was there brought me such comfort. This was never more obvious to me than when he was no longer there. That home didn't feel the same. Even though my mom was still there, the anchor, the cornerstone, the one who gave it foundation and stability was gone.

You may not have an earthly dad who brings you that kind of security and comfort. If so, I'm sorry, my sister. I can only imagine the hole in your soul that loss represents. However, you have a heavenly Father who loves you perfectly, and it is His presence and the certainty that Jesus has prepared a place for you in His house that can help bring your soul stability.

Jesus used figurative language to communicate what our dwelling with God will be like.

> Which phrase below best represents how Jesus described our Father's house (John 14:2)?
>
> ☐ unending luxury suites
> ☑ many rooms
> ☐ several small cabins

In most modern translations (CSB, NIV, ESV, NASB), it says there are *many rooms* in the Father's house. But in the KJV, *mansions* was how it was translated. So, maybe you've grown up thinking we get a palatial dwelling with opulence and a coffee bar! (Okay, the coffee bar is my idea of Heaven.) That wasn't the point Jesus was making, though.

What do you think Jesus meant?

The Greek word for *house* in the phrase *my Father's house* is *tē oikia*, which can be used to communicate a physical house or a family.[4] Hmm. Perhaps the message here is not about rooms or mansions or dwelling places but about identity and family? You belong. I belong. There is plenty of room. We are family, and we have a home.

Oh, my friend, whatever wonder our eyes have seen here dims in light of what God has prepared for us there. Whatever beauty I imagine in the hue of a blue flower is sepia tone compared to the radiance that will burst forth before my seeing, enlightened eyes in Heaven.

So, we begin this study by acknowledging the great mystery of Christ crucified, raised, and glorified, and we anticipate the great mystery of seeing Him face to face someday— when our faith becomes sight.

Through the coming pages of this study, we'll pick apart Scripture to understand truths about our glorious unending, our risen life after death. But why we do this needs to be super clear.

So, let's end there. Why think about Heaven?

What reason did Jesus give to His disciples in **John 14:1**?

☐ To clarify their mission
☐ To correct their theology
☑ To comfort their hearts

Our compassionate Savior knew the troubled hearts of His disciples needed comfort. His words about His Father's house affirmed and assured them of the truth that there was far more to this life than the uncertainty they felt. This same truth can untrouble our hearts, too.

Consider your heart for a moment. Does it have some troubled spots?

Jot down what is unsettling you. Then ask God to use your growing understanding and anticipation of Heaven to bring comfort to your troubled heart.

My Troubled Heart List

Pause and write a prayer, pouring your heart out to Jesus.

Dear God,

Amen

(In a few weeks, we'll revisit this list to see how your troubled heart is being affected by what you are learning about Heaven.)

All right, we're done for now, so go pick a blue flower (or find a picture of one) and study the fragile strength of each perfectly designed petal. Physically or imaginatively breathe in its fragrance and cast your gaze far past it to that place, the place God has prepared for you, the daughter He loves. Be comforted and strengthened today.

Tomorrow, ice cream. Really.

" . . . and I will dwell in the house of the Lord forever."

PSALM 23:6

The Scoop on Heaven

"One drop of the sweetness of Heaven is enough to take away all the sourness
and bitterness of all the afflictions in the world."[5]

JEREMIAH BURROUGHS

Pull up a chair, because we're going to get the scoop on Heaven today, and it will be sweeter than ice cream!

But before we start, let's ask God's Spirit to "open our eyes" so we may know the hope to which we are called.

Thank You, Lord, for our inheritance in Christ and in each other.
Teach us today about our glorious unending in Your presence.
Amen (Eph. 1:18).

Let me start by asking you some questions.

Where did King David, Ruth, Ezekiel, Deborah, and other Old Testament people go when they died? After all, Jesus hadn't come yet. Had He prepared the place in His Father's house for them?

Or what about the thief who hung on the cross next to Jesus? Where did he go the day Jesus promised him they would be together in Paradise?

Where did Peter, Paul, Mary Magdalene, and other New Testament believers who died after Jesus was resurrected end up?

And what happens to all of them and us after Jesus returns? What is our final destination? Will we be in the same place they're in right now?

Whew.

Underline the statement below that best represents your response to those questions?

- Never thought about it.

- Uh, I'm confused.

- I have a working understanding of where Old and New Testament saints went when they died.

- What? I just want to focus on the promise of Heaven rather than getting into those weeds.

- Dude, it's all Heaven. Don't get so picky.

Before I studied about Heaven, I thought it was just the place where God dwells and where I go when I die. I thought I'd show up there; get a new body; see Jesus, my dad, and C. S. Lewis; and not be blind. That was pretty much the extent of my thinking.

And oh, how I wanted all of that. Heaven felt like relief to me. It was rescue from the prison of my blind body, freedom to know and be known and be me.

I never thought to ask those questions.

What about you? What are your thoughts about Heaven? Is it appealing to you or not? Explain.

What helped form your impressions of Heaven? Books? Songs? Scriptures?

I grew up singing a song that proclaimed I had a mansion just over the hilltop where I would walk streets of gold and never grow old. But now I wonder. *Really? Is that true?*

I realized how little I understood about Heaven, and what I assumed about it was a little egocentric and a lot informed by songs as much as Scripture. Quite honestly, all the confusion I felt about Heaven troubled my heart.

So, as we begin digging into the details about Heaven, with some that may be new to you, don't let them shake you or diminish your view. Instead, let them bring clarity. Trust me, the process will help you love God deeply, long for Heaven more, and live on earth with an untroubled heart.

Alright, here we go.

What does the Bible actually say about Heaven?

First, when you read the word *Heaven* in the Bible, it has one of three meanings.

1. Where the bluebird flies. This is the air within earth's atmosphere (Deut. 4:17; Matt. 6:26).

2. Where the sun, moon, and stars are. The expanse of the universe (Gen. 1:1,17; Ps. 19:1-2).

3. The dwelling place of God (1 Kings 8:39; Matt. 6:9; Phil. 3:20).

So, don't assume every time you read the word *Heaven* in the Bible, it is referring to our eternal home with God. In fact, there are several words used in the Bible to represent Heaven and our afterlife with God.

Read the following passages and write the word used to represent Heaven in each one.

2 Kings 2:11 _Elijah went in a whirlwind._

Luke 16:19-31 _Lazarus was carried by angels to Abraham's side._

Luke 23:43 _Paradise_

2 Corinthians 5:1 _Eternal house_

2 Corinthians 12:2 _Third heaven_

Hebrews 11:16 _City_

All these words for Heaven have different contexts and connotations we will explore more as we go along. But let's start thinking of all of this as one sweet treat from God—a carton of Neapolitan ice cream! You're welcome.

Growing up, every time I went to my southern grandmother's house, she served up Neapolitan ice cream in the daintiest pink parfaits! She always gave me three scoops—chocolate on the bottom, vanilla in the middle, and strawberry on top. You know what Neapolitan ice cream looks like, right? It's a carton of yummy, creamy delight in three flavors: chocolate, vanilla, and strawberry. Of course, this imagery is not scriptural, and I'm not using it as an analogy; it's just a fun, illustrative way to serve up some clarity about Heaven.

Even though we think of Heaven as ultimately one place, we need to see how the Scripture talks about it in three different time periods.

If this were Neapolitan ice cream, these would be the three scoops:

Scoop 1: This would be chocolate. It's how the Bible speaks of pre-resurrection Heaven—from creation to the cross.

Scoop 2: This would be the vanilla. It's how the Bible speaks of post-resurrection Heaven—from the empty tomb to the return of Christ.

Scoop 3: This would be strawberry. This is how Scripture describes post-return Heaven—from the return of Christ to the rest of forever.

Pause and read those again. Ask God to help you get that clear in your mind before we go on. To establish the foundation of our understanding, fill in the timeline below, labeling each section according to those three scoops. And if you're creative, you can make it look like Neapolitan ice cream.

| Chocolate | Vanilla | Strawberry |

This week we'll get a tiny taste of all three, but today let's start with chocolate, because that's a fine way to start! In fact, if you want to go grab some of that frozen delight (educational purposes only, of course), go ahead. I'll wait!

Again, you're welcome.

FIRST SCOOP OF HEAVEN

This is the far-left side of your timeline. It's pre-resurrection, the time between creation and the cross, specifically the time of the Old Testament.

> Where does the Old Testament say followers of God went when they died? Read the following verses and jot down the words used to describe what happened to Abraham and Jacob when they died.
>
> **Genesis 15:15**
>
>
>
> **Genesis 49:29**

When Abraham and Jacob died, Scripture indicates they went to "their ancestors (or fathers) in peace." They were gathered to their people.

That tells us the company they kept but not where they went. What was their location?

> Read **Genesis 37:35; 42:38**. Where did Jacob say his final destination would be?
>
> His grave

Sheol (the grave). What and where is it? You may have thought, like me, that Sheol was another name for Hell. There's more to it than that. Let me give you a brief (as opposed to exhaustive) explanation.

In the Old Testament, the word *Sheol* was used to refer simply to the grave or to the place of the dead. It seems all were destined to experience it (Ps. 89:48). While it was definitely seen as the place the wicked were consigned to (Ps. 9:17; 49:13-14), it was also spoken of as the place the righteous went when they died. We already heard Jacob mention it, proclaiming he would "surely go down to Sheol" (Gen. 37:35). Job described it as "the land of darkness and gloom" where he would go and never return (Job 10:21). That sounds hopeless. But that theme of never returning seems to be more about not escaping death, rather than being confined there for eternity. Sheol may have been a place of the dead but not a dead end. The Old Testament writers hinted at this hope.

Read the following passages and note the hope expressed by each writer.

Job 19:25-27

He knew he would see God.

Psalm 49:15; 86:13

Temple assistants - God would redeem.
David - God had delivered him from the grave.

Isaiah 26:19

The dead will live.

So at this point in Scripture, all people go to the place of the dead when they die. But there are hints of separation and a different experience between the righteous and the unrighteous.

Now, stay with me; this is going to make sense! By the time of the New Testament, the after-life experience and location for the righteous and unrighteous was better defined, as seen in one of Jesus's parables.

Read **Luke 16:19-31** and answer the questions below.

Where did Lazarus and the rich man go when they died?

Lazarus - Abraham's side
Rich man - Hell

In this parable, could they see each other?

Yes

How did Jesus describe what separated Lazarus and the rich man?

Lazarus received bad things so was being comforted.
Rich man experienced good things on earth

Two things we must keep in mind: 1) The main point of this parable was not to give a physical description of the afterlife; 2) building a doctrine based on a parable is asking too much of the story. However, the parable does illustrate Jewish thought at the time of Jesus about the place where the dead are located. Also, Jesus would not tell a story that was false. It would at least have echoes of the truth.

The parable depicts a realm with compartments.

What are the two compartments?

_____*Hades*_____ and _____*Abraham's side*_____

In the parable, Hades represented a place of separation and punishment for the unrighteous, while Abraham's bosom (side) represented a place where the righteous dead experienced comfort and communion with God. For them, it was a blessed state of existence after death. So, before Jesus's death and resurrection, Scripture indicates all who died went to the place of the dead, where the righteous and unrighteous have a conscious existence but are separated and having very different experiences. They are in a holding pattern, you might say, waiting for what's to come next.

Hopefully this illustration helps:

CREATION TO CROSS
(Pre-resurrection Understanding of Life after Death)

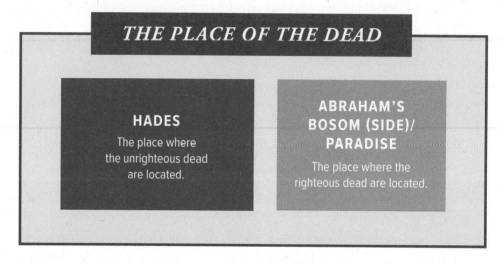

Whew! Do you have brain freeze yet? I hope not! I know this may have been a lot to swallow, but it helps us get a taste so we can keep getting the scoop on Heaven.

Maybe you learned, or unlearned, something today that you never knew or thought about. I hope it was as satisfying as chocolate!

Before you finish up today, pray Psalm 86:10-13.

> *O God, your love toward your people is unwavering and astounding. Thank You for delivering our souls from the depths of sorrow, the depths of sin, the depths of self, and the depths of Sheol. We praise You in Jesus's name. Amen!*

Good job, sister!

Tomorrow, another scoop: vanilla!

DAY 3

Ain't No Plain Vanilla Here!

*"When a mortal man speaks anything of that eternal blessedness of the saints
in glory, he is like a blind man discoursing about the light which he has never
seen, and so cannot distinctly speak anything concerning it."*[6]

CHARLES H. SPURGEON

All right, we enjoyed a big scoop of chocolate yesterday. We got a taste of how Scripture speaks of the afterlife between creation and the cross. This gave us an understanding of where both the righteous and unrighteous dead went before Christ's resurrection. To refresh your memory, flip back to page 24 and look at the timeline you created yesterday. When you do, note that today we will be in the vanilla of our Neapolitan ice cream. This is the second scoop of Heaven, looking at how Scripture talks about Heaven from Christ's resurrection to Christ's return.

Now that you've got that image in your mind, take a deep breath, relax your mind, open your heart, and ask God's Holy Spirit to guide you into truth today.

> *Thank You, Lord, for Your Spirit who teaches us and guides us into truth. Teach us today for Christ's glory and our good. Amen (John 16:13).*

This may be the vanilla flavor of our Neapolitan ice cream, but trust me, it's not plain! This scoop of Heaven is now—the time between Jesus's resurrection and His return.

Read **2 Corinthians 12:2-4** and jot down the two titles Paul gives what I call this second scoop of Heaven.

Third heaven and paradise

Paul seems to be using *third Heaven* and *Paradise* synonymously. This is the only place the third Heaven is mentioned in the Bible.

What do you think Paul means by this? Is there a first and second Heaven?

Yesterday we saw that *Heaven* can mean one of three things in Scripture (p. 24). The third Heaven is referring to the highest Heaven, the place where God dwells, in contrast to where the birds fly and the planets rotate.

Paradise is used only two other places in Scripture to describe Heaven. Let's take a look.

Read **Luke 23:32-43**.

What did Jesus say to the thief who hung next to Him?

He didn't tell him he'd have to pass through two layers of Heaven and then eventually he'd be there. No.

"Today you will be with me in paradise."

What can you deduce about Heaven from those eight words Jesus spoke to the thief?

Jesus knew the thief wasn't going to make it off the cross alive that day, so His use of the word *today* suggests that to be dead here is to be alive there. And Jesus saying *with me*, indicates the thief and Jesus would be together in the same place. And the name of this place: *Paradise*.

Now find **Revelation 2:7**.

What can you deduce about Paradise based on this verse?

Paradise is the place where the tree of life flourishes and nourishes. The victorious Christ follower will have the right to eat from it. So evidently, Paradise is vibrant, alive, and for the living.

Both Paradise and the third Heaven describe a place prepared for Christ's family: a place of reward, revelation, and rest.

One phrase we will use to describe this second scoop of Heaven not found in Scripture is "intermediate state."

> If you are ambitious, grab your favorite Bible resource or just search the internet for "intermediate state." Summarize what you find.

The intermediate state, put simply, is the time between a person's bodily death and their bodily resurrection. For believers in Christ, the intermediate state is a time of conscious existence in Paradise, or the present Heaven, separated from their physical bodies.

> How do we know this?

> Read **Philippians 1:21-24**. What internal struggle was Paul dealing with?

> What did Paul consider to be his better choice?

> How would that be better?

Paul desired to depart to be with Christ. If Paul were to fade into unconscious oblivion when he died, would that be better? I think not. If Paul were in some spiritual limbo state until the resurrection, would that be better? No. In neither case would there be fellowship with Christ.

> For Paul, departing this life and arriving in the presence of Christ was better than staying in his earthly life. Does that feel like the better choice to you? Why or why not? Be honest.

It's okay if it doesn't feel better to you yet. After all, departing means leaving your loved ones here. And if we're honest, lots of us have some degree of a fear of death. We might say we're spiritually prepared to go to Heaven; we're just not volunteering to go today! I get it. My prayer for you, for us, is that we will have such a clear revelation of Heaven—being with Christ and our glorious unending—that leaving earth will not feel like loss but gain. So be patient with yourself and the process of God's Spirit preparing you.

Moving on.

Let's take another look at Paul expressing his desire to be with Christ.

> Read **2 Corinthians 5:6-8**.
>
> Explain in your own words the truth Paul was confident about.

> What was Paul's preferred option (v. 8)?

Paul desired to be away from his human body and be with Christ. He was sure that the moment he left this life he would be fully alive, aware in Christ's presence. We also can be sure that the day we become absent from these human bodies, we will be fully alive in the presence of the Lord.

Alright, you're doing great. Let's look at one more Scripture passage to help us grasp this concept.

> Read **Revelation 6:9-10**. How are the deceased believers described. Where are they and what are they doing?

John described these martyred believers as "souls" who were positioned under the altar and were actively "crying out" to the Lord. They are fully alive in God's presence and animated, even if not with the same kind of body we are familiar with here and now.

We will learn more about this in a few weeks. But for now, what we need to understand is that from post-resurrection until Christ's return, the New Testament indicates that those believers who die exist in an intermediate state in the present Heaven with Him. They are absent from their earthly bodies and present with the Lord in Paradise.

They are not in a suspended state of sleep. It is not an unconscious existence. No. They are fully alive in God's presence.

This is where my dad is. This is where your deceased loved ones who know Christ are. And if you know Jesus, this is where you will go if you die before Christ's return.

I told you this would be no plain vanilla, right?

These may be new thoughts for you. It may make you feel a little insecure about what you know, what you think you know, and what you may need to learn and unlearn. I realize the more I know, the more I need to know, and there may be things we cannot know.

> Let's close by reviewing **2 Corinthians 12:2-4**. As you read it, note or circle each time Paul admits he does not know. And what phrase does Paul use after he says that he does not know?

God knows.

Did you catch that, my friend? Paul, who was caught up into Heaven, into the presence of God, admitted he didn't know if it was in the body or apart from the body. He says he Did. Not. Know.

Can we be okay with admitting there are things we don't know either? And can we also rest on the two words Paul repeated twice: God knows?

He does know, my friend. He knows your questions, your confusion, your concerns. He knows you, and He loves you. Let not your heart be troubled. Cast your eyes past the shadows of this life to that bright beautiful forever God has for you.

"For now we see in a mirror dimly, but then face to face."

1 CORINTHIANS 13:12 (NASB)

All right. Well done, sister. Tomorrow, our last scoop of Heaven—an endless scoop of strawberry!

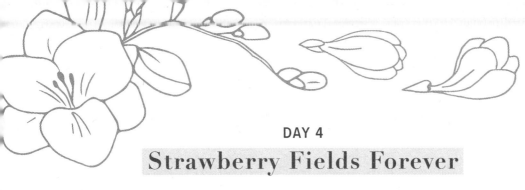

DAY 4

Strawberry Fields Forever

"If you're a child of God, you do not just 'go around once' on Earth. You don't get just one earthly life. You get another—one far better and without end. You'll inhabit the New Earth! You'll live with the God you cherish and the people you love as an undying person on an undying Earth."[7]

RANDY ALCORN

It's just after sunrise, and I'm sitting on the deck. The simple grandeur of Table Rock Lake spreads out before me echoing an unending "ta-da!" Of course, I can't see it, but oh, how it draws all my senses to its presence. The subtle fragrance of pine. The symphony of birds. The gentle caress of the breeze. The serene march of the water. All are like seeds of a blue flower planted deep in my heart, blossoming into a beautiful ache for forever.

As I sit breathing it in, it feels like it goes on and on—no boundaries, just beauty that lasts forever. Of course, I know there is a city somewhere lurking at the edges of this mini paradise. But if you could sit here with me, close your eyes and just take it in, I think you would feel it too. And as I sit here, I wonder: is this what it feels like when our glorious unending begins? Will it be so sensory rich and satisfying that we need forever just to absorb a tiny piece of it?

If you could design your "forever," what would it be like?

We long for a forever so satisfying that even the ache for it brings us deep joy. We are created by God with this longing because only God can satisfy it. This ache begins to find satisfaction in our glorious unending in the new earth, which is our third scoop of Heaven.

I hope you came with a big appetite, because this is the strawberry flavor of our Neapolitan ice cream, and this last scoop is your glorious unending, which will go on and on forever!

Let's go back once again to the timeline you filled in on page 24. Or better yet, draw it here and review.

This strawberry scoop is the "post-return" scoop of Heaven. It's how the New Testament talks about Heaven after Christ returns. It's when the in-between becomes the glorious unending, when the intermediate state gives way to our permanent state, when our blessed hope is finally made sight in our ultimate home where all Christ's redeemed get glorified resurrection bodies and live on the new earth.

We'll dive more deeply into the details about the new earth in Session Five, but for now let's get a taste of what's to come.

Read **Revelation 21:3-5** and then pause and pray.

Lord, help us, your children, to get a glimpse of what you have prepared for us. Thank You that you will dwell among us, You will be our God, and we will be Your people in the new earth forever. Amen (Rev. 21:3-5).

Let's see in Scripture how this third and final scoop gets served up. And you may want some kind of pink drink to sip as you study, so go grab it!

Read **John 6:40**, and summarize what Jesus said.

Based on that verse, what is Jesus going to do on the last day for those who believe in Him?

☐ Wake them up.
☐ Raise them up.
☐ Save them.

Oh, my friend, on the "last day," Jesus won't sound some kind of cosmic alarm clock waking up those who died in Christ, because their souls are not asleep! And He won't save those who died, because that matter was concluded when they were alive. No. Jesus promised that He would raise up the believers' bodies.

Let's get a picture of what He meant by the "last day" and raising us up.

Note that "last day" is also referred to in Scripture as "that day."

> Beside each of the following references, write what Scripture teaches about the last day and how we are supposed to live today as we look forward to it.
>
> **Romans 13:11-14**
>
>
>
> **Philippians 1:6**
>
>
>
> **2 Timothy 1:12**
>
>
>
> **2 Timothy 4:8**
>
>
>
> **Hebrews 10:24-25**

The return of Christ is considered "that day" or "the last day" or "the day of Christ." That truly will be a glorious day! But it seems the New Testament writers were just as concerned about how we live presently as we wait for that day.

We are to clothe ourselves in the armor of light and walk in godliness as God works to complete His work in us. We walk in assurance knowing He is able to guard what we have trusted to Him, and we anticipate the crown waiting for us on that day. And we need to continue to meet together and encourage each other as that day approaches.

Don't you love that?

> Pause and reflect. How are you living this day in light of that day? Do any of those verses strike you as something you need, by God's Spirit and grace, to apply to live this day well? Journal your thoughts.

Let's take a minute and look to the future "that day"! What should we expect to happen on that last day?

> Read **1 Thessalonians 4:16–17**. Based on those verses, create a list in order of what happens when Christ returns.

1. _____

2. _____

3. _____

4. _____

5. _____

Notice these two items on your list: The dead in Christ will rise and those who remain alive will be caught up to meet Jesus on that day. In this passage Paul stated that those believers who are in the intermediate state, their bodies are raised up first. Then, if we are still kicking down here, we get caught up also.

Look at how John states it in **1 John 3:2**.

Beautiful, right?

> Now read **2 Peter 3:12-13**, and describe what Peter says happens on that day.

Oh, my friend, we are promised new heavens and new earth (v. 13)! We will inhabit the new earth as Christ's redeemed people. This is our eternal state.

Someday earth will be made new, according to God's Edenic intent, and we will dwell there forever with Him and each other.

It's hard to imagine how all this goes down or comes up! But as we already said, God knows, and we can trust Him with His calendar and our future.

> For me, the big takeaway is at the end of **1 Thessalonians 4:17**. Look at it again. Jot down the promise found in the last phrase.

> What are your emotions and thoughts as you meditate on this promise?

Always. Forever. That's how long we will be with the Lord. It's how "that day" ends—with our glorious unending with Jesus on the new earth!

I remember the day my dad overheard me singing, "This world is not my home, I'm just passing through." He waited at my bedroom door until I finished the last line, "and I can't feel at home in this world anymore."[8] Then he walked in my room and reminded me I was only eight years old, so I needed to figure out a way to feel at home here in my yellow bedroom with my Barbie® dolls! He mussed my hair, and we both laughed.

I just liked the melody. I didn't think about the lyrics at all.

But now, as a grown-up, I wonder, maybe this world is my home after all? Just not in its present sin-stained, fallen state. Some Bible scholars believe the new heavens and new earth will be completely new, and some believe the earth will be completely restored—*made* new. I lean toward the latter. I believe this world—this earth that awakens all my senses when I sit on the deck overlooking Table Rock Lake—is the same earth that will be made new. Just as we await "the redemption of our bodies" (Rom. 8:23), all creation, which God originally declared good back in Genesis 1, is also waiting for redemption. As Paul said in Romans 8:20-21 (CSB),

> "For the creation was subjected to futility—not willingly, but because
> of him who subjected it—in the hope that the creation itself will also
> be set free from the bondage to decay into the glorious freedom of
> God's children."

I love the way Randy Alcorn states it: "It will be as if an artist wiped away the old paint, stained and cracking, and started a new and better painting, but using the same images on the same canvas."[9] Earth will be restored and fit for God Himself to dwell among us, His redeemed children, where there will be no more tears or pain.

The beauty becomes more breathtaking. The joy becomes deeper. The curtains on the window of forever will be flung open wide so we will see with enlightened eyes our glorious unending! And perhaps there will be endless fields of blue flowers! Thank You, Lord.

So if that last day is a glorious day that ushers in forever days on the new earth, what are we to do with that truth besides look forward to it?

What is the concluding application Paul adds in **1 Thessalonians 4:18**?

How can you be encouraged or give encouragement based on
1 Thessalonians 4:16-17? What are the implications for your troubled
heart list on page 19?

Well, sister, the ice cream carton is empty! This day of study has probably answered some questions you had and created more. I get it. Let's be patient with the process as we study and build our understanding of Heaven. I also realize it's difficult to do a study of Heaven without end times questions rearing their cute, controversial, and confusing heads!

But the point of this study is what happens when we die, where we go, and what the Bible teaches about our forever risen life. It's not an end times study. My view on end times might be different from your view, but that's okay. We can still agree on the forever outcome.

Let's honor God's Word that He gave to the apostle Paul. Let's comfort each other with these things, not criticize each other. Comfort and encourage each other with the main thing: we will always be with the Lord.

Pray the concluding statement in Revelation 22:20-21 as we finish up.

Amen! Come, Lord Jesus!

Grace and peace to you, my friend.

Tomorrow is your first *Takeaway Truths* and *Dash Living Day*.

Love,

Jennifer

TAKEAWAY TRUTHS

Below are some important points we covered this week. There's also room for you to add other takeaways you want to remember.

- If you know Christ as Savior and Lord, you have an eternal home with Him that is secure.

- Before Christ's death and resurrection, Scripture indicates all who died, both righteous and unrighteous, went to the place of the dead (Sheol). There they have a conscious existence but are in separate places—unrighteous in Hades, righteous in Paradise (Abraham's side).

- The intermediate state is the time between a person's death and bodily resurrection. Believers, upon their deaths, will immediately go to be with the Lord in Paradise/Heaven.

- There is a day in the future when Jesus will return. At that point, believers will receive resurrected bodies and forever live with God on the new earth.

YOUR DASH VALUES

List below what matters most to you as you live within the dashes—the time between your birth and death—and share why you place value on those items. (If you need more space, feel free to use paper or a digital journal.)

In the present, this can serve as a compass to guide you as you navigate life on this side of eternity. It can help you evaluate your priorities, making sure you're giving time, resources, and attention to what's really important to you.

In the future, after your faith becomes sight and you are in the presence of the Lord, the people you leave behind will have a clear understanding of what was important to you. They can use your list as source material to write your eulogy or obituary. Or maybe it just makes for interesting conversation about you around the dinner table. Even from the grave you can influence their conversation!

MY DASH VALUES

WHAT I VALUE	WHY

"How much better to get wisdom than gold, to get insight rather than silver!"

PROVERBS 16:16

LIVING AN 8:18 LIFE

21 - 23

BEFORE THE VIDEO

JAMES 4:1

Welcome and Prayer

WATCH THE VIDEO

THREE Cs FROM ROMANS 8:18

1. *CONSIDER*

   • Consider if suffering is because of ____*SIN*____ .

   • Consider if suffering is because of *CIRCUMSTANCE*

2. *COMPARE*

   • We compare this present suffering to the ____*GLORY*____ that will be revealed.

   • Let the ____*GOOD*____ lead to glory.

   • Let the *GROANS* lead to glory.

3. *CONTEMPLATE*

   • The glory will be revealed ____*IN*____ us and ____*TO*____ us.

GLORY = WEIGHT

GRAVITY OF GOD

Go to **jenniferrothschild.com/heaven** to get a summary of this video teaching sent to your inbox. And listen to my *Heaven* playlist to keep your heart encouraged and connected to Heaven.

2 COR 4: 16-18

To access the video teaching sessions, use the instructions in the back of your Bible study book.

CONVERSATION GUIDE

PERSONAL BIBLE STUDY

- Which was your favorite day of study? Why?

- Is there anything in your life, past or present, that stirs in you a desire for Heaven? Should there be?

- What are the implications of Jesus calling Heaven "my Father's House"? What emotions or thoughts does that title stir in you?

- What did you learn and unlearn about Heaven from this week of study?

- For Paul, dying and going to be with Christ was better than staying alive on earth. Do you feel the same way? Explain.

- Is what Scripture teaches about the last day, when Jesus returns, currently affecting how you live this day? Explain.

- Which *Takeaway Truth* stands out to you and why?

- *Dash Living Day*: What are some things you listed on your Dash Values list and why?

VIDEO TEACHING

- What's one thing that stood out to you from the video teaching? Why?

- Why is it important for us to consider our suffering?

- How would you define *glory*?

- What does it mean to compare our sufferings? What are we comparing them to? Is that difficult to do? Explain.

- How can both the good and the groans lead to glory? Is that happening in your life? Explain.

- How is glory going to be revealed both to us and in us?

SESSION TWO

"He has made everything beautiful in its time. He has also set eternity in the human heart; yet no one can fathom what God has done from beginning to end. I know that there is nothing better for people than to be happy and to do good while they live. That each of them may eat and drink, and find satisfaction in all their toil—this is the gift of God. I know that everything God does will endure forever; nothing can be added to it and nothing taken from it. God does it so that people will fear him. Whatever is has already been, and what will be has been before; and God will call the past to account."

ECCLESIASTES 3:11-15

ETERNITY IN YOUR HEART

This week, we'll clearly see we weren't made for this life, but for eternity. We'll deal with the stark reality of Hell and see how the Bible speaks of it throughout its pages. The harsh reality of Hell will lead us to examine the hope found in the gospel. This week of study ends with an examination of eternal rewards for those who've trusted Christ. So, get set for a reality check, some sobering study, but then some really good news!

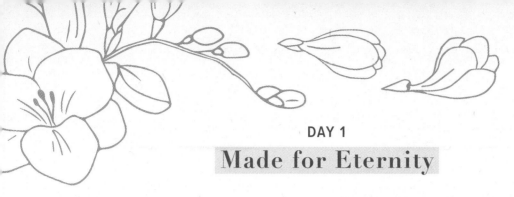

Made for Eternity

"We have the hunger for eternity in our souls, the thought of eternity in our hearts, the destination for eternity written on our inmost being, and the need to ally ourselves with eternity proclaimed by the most short-lived trifles of time."[1]

ALEXANDER MACLAREN

We are in our second week, and since we're all friends now, I want to invite you into my living room with my hubby and me. We'd just finished dinner and were watching the evening news together.

"I'm not that into longevity."

My husband, Phil, looked over at me, all wrapped up in a blanket on the loveseat, and asked, "Did he say what I think he said?" I wondered the same when I heard it.

The news anchor was discussing a newly approved drug, and evidently this anchor's doctor recommended the news guy take it to help improve his health. The anchor commented that he wasn't comfortable with the possible side effects and then concluded, "Besides, I'm not that into longevity anyway."

Phil rewound to make sure we heard it correctly. We'd just never heard anyone say anything like that so comfortably. Yep, that is exactly what he said.

As I brushed my teeth that night and went through my seven steps of cleansing, steaming, exfoliating, toning, moisturizing, oiling, and praying over my aging face, I couldn't get his words out of my mind. I wondered, *am I that into longevity*? Well, clearly, I was into the longevity of the skin on my face—wanting it to hold up as long as I do!

Living a long, satisfying life here is a desirable and good thing. And if you are in your twenties, thirties, forties—well, just about any decade—you are fired up to live on this earth with all your people as long as you can. And you should feel that way. Life is good, and we should seek to live it as well and as long as possible. Yet, we weren't made simply for longevity; we were made for eternity.

Now, before we dig into that last phrase, let's be clear. We are not eternal. We did not exist before we were born here. Only God is eternal, with no beginning and no end (Ps. 90:2). You and me? We had a beginning; yet, we will live eternally.

Let's ask God to teach us today as we pray together.

Lord, You are high and exalted, inhabiting eternity. Your name is holy. We humble ourselves before You and ask You to revive our spirits and teach us Your truth. Amen (Isa. 57:15).

Now let's get a glimpse of our own longevity according to Scripture.

Personalize a description of your life and longevity based on the following verses and use words like "I" and "my." I've done the first one to help you get started.

Psalm 39:4 *Lord, help me clearly see that my days are numbered so I can understand how short my life is.*

Psalm 90:10 The length of my days is unknown + they quickly pass

Psalm 139:16 The number of my days were written in your book before one came to be.

Psalm 144:4 Like a breath our days are a fleeting shadow.

Ecclesiastes 3:1-2 A time to be born and a time to die

Hebrews 9:27 When you die, you will face judgement.

Once you've finished, read your list out loud. Summarize what you just said about yourself.

According to those verses, you have a birth date and a death date. All your days are ordained by God, and He has them recorded. You may live to be seventy or eighty years old, but those days will pass as quickly as a fleeting shadow. You have an appointment with death; it is your destiny, so you need the Lord to show you how fleeting your days really are.

What are your emotions and thoughts surrounding the truth you just discovered? How do you feel about your own longevity? Jot down your honest thoughts and include the why.

You may consider yourself young. And by the way, whatever your current age, you're as young as you will ever be. My point is, wherever you are in your timeline—college student, young single, newlywed, have small kids, empty nest, or recently retired—all those life stages can feel young. And of course, you want to live as long and as fulfilling a life as possible.

But I want you to consider that you are made for even more. Let's turn our hearts toward eternity by turning to **Ecclesiastes 3:11**.

Hold your place there for a sec.

It seems that every culture, every civilization, in every century demonstrates an awareness that there is something beyond longevity. Eternity.

The ancient Egyptians believed that after death their souls lived on in a blissful existence in the Field of Reeds. Their bodies were mummified for the journey, and they made sure they were buried with all the trinkets they would need for their afterlife.

The Greeks put their hope in the myth that they would end up frolicking in the Elysian Fields if they made the cut in this life.

The ancient Mesopotamians envisioned an after-death underworld thought of as the Land of No Return.

Ancient Chinese practiced ancestral veneration, the act of showing respect or honor to their dead ancestors whom they believed had power to bring influence and blessings to living descendants.

Buddhism believes in reincarnation, and Taoism teaches multiple realms of existence for wandering spirits after death.

> Now read **Ecclesiastes 3:11** and ponder: what do all those beliefs about the afterlife have in common?

It seems most people, regardless of culture or religion, believe there is more than just this life. Why? God has placed eternity into our hearts.

The most common interpretation of this verse is that God has placed an eternal longing, or a sense of eternity, in our souls. In my words, He has planted the seeds of the blue flower in us that will grow and blossom!

Yet here we are, made for eternity but bound by time. As we read earlier in Ecclesiastes 3:1, time exists, and there is a time for everything.

> Now read the next seven verses in **Ecclesiastes 3** and note the contrasts Solomon pointed out in each one. Pick a few of them and jot down a personal example of how that specific time or season has shown up in your life.

Verse 2 To be born + die

Verse 3 To tear down + rebuild

Verse 4 Weep + laugh

Verse 5 Embrace + restrain

Verse 6 Keep + throw away

Verse 7 *Tear down & mend*

Verse 8 *Love + hate*

Life is full of opposite experiences, isn't it? And there is a time for each one.

Yet, Solomon started Ecclesiastes with a sobering thesis concerning all the shifting sands of time and our days here.

> Read **Ecclesiastes 1:2**. What was Solomon's thesis?
>
> ☐ It's all difficult.
> ☑ It's all meaningless.
> ☐ It's all helpful.
> ☐ It's all satisfying.

Meaningless. Really?

> The KJV translates *meaningless* as *vanity*. Write a dictionary definition of vanity.

Vanity suggests that something has a lack of real value. It's worthless, trivial, or pointless.

Think about your list of personal examples you recorded earlier. Were all those things pointless? Worthless?

The birth of my kids was not meaningless, nor was the death of my dad. Moments of laughter and grief, celebrating success, and uprooting our family for a move, work, and relationships. None were pointless. Vanity? Certainly not.

> So what do you think Solomon could have meant by that statement in **Ecclesiastes 1:2**?

Perhaps he meant that in and of themselves, without the grounding and context of eternity, all that stuff will never ever satisfy. Those temporal things add to our joy in this life, but they do not compose our eternal satisfaction.

Life and time are vanity without certainty of eternity.

How did James describe our lives in James 4:14?

Live for God today

Compared to eternity, our current life here is like a mist that appears and is gone, whether it lasts seventeen years or seventy years. But thankfully, our risen life is not a vapor. It is vast and long and unending.

We were not made to be just vapor people. We had finite beginnings, but we were created as eternal souls with eternity in our hearts and eternity in our futures.

Back to the loveseat with Phil and me watching the news. I knew a little about that news anchor's life and assumed he was a man of faith based on comments he had made in the past. So, I wondered, maybe he isn't so concerned about longevity because he is so comfortable with eternity?

Are you?

Study your heart. Earlier you wrote your thoughts about longevity. Now, how do you feel about eternity? Journal your thoughts.

A place of perfection

If you have questions or concerns about living forever, jot them down somewhere so you can talk about them with your Bible study buddies. We will also probably tackle some of those questions in Session Four.

For now, consider this: the more comfortable we get with eternity, the less concerned we'll be about longevity.

If that's the case, then our lives will not be lived in vain, but will be filled with quality days that prepare us for that glorious day when our faith becomes sight.

Well, we're done for now. But oh, get ready for tomorrow. The Marines have Hell Week, but we're going to have Hell Day. I know, no fun. But we can't talk candidly about eternity and Heaven without getting honest and clear about what the Bible says about Hell.

Until then, meditate on **Psalm 31:14-15**, and make it a prayer to the God who holds you and is strong to deliver you.

"But I trust in you, LORD; I say, 'You are my God.'
My times are in your hands."

PSALM 31:14-15a

Good job today!

Bad News: Hell is Real

"There are only two kinds of people in the end: those who say to God, 'Thy will be done,' and those to whom God says, in the end: 'Thy will be done.' All that are in Hell, choose it. Without that self-choice there could be no Hell."[2]

C. S. LEWIS

I'll start with some inside scoop on me and then I want you to share. When I don't like an upcoming task and I don't want to do it, I call it "unfun" and procrastinate as much as humanly possible. For example, since I've pulled up my chair to my desk to write about Hell this morning (a subject I consider highly unfun) I've checked the status of an online order, cleaned out my desk drawer, changed my pants because the waist feels way too snug to sit here, searched the internet for the symptoms of TMJ because I just noticed my jaws are aching, researched if peppermint oil helps deter insects (because now I'm itching), and organized my iPhone® charging cables from longest to shortest. In between all that, I've brewed two more cups of coffee, determined standing at my desk is healthier, and checked my weather app.

> How about you? When something is unfun and you don't want to deal with it, how do you handle it?

Well, sister, Hell is one of the subjects that qualifies as totally, completely, unalterably unfun. But we need to deal with it. So go ahead and check on your online shopping order, organize your desk drawer, pour your coffee, and do all the things so you can show up one hundred percent to do this.

First, a caution. When it comes to talking about something unfun, we could ease our discomfort by trying to be funny or we could make this awkward subject a little more palatable by trivializing it. However, we won't do either. Hell is real, it isn't funny, and it's one of the most consequential doctrines in Scripture. But that does not mean that we will not also experience hope as we study, so let's ask God to guide us today.

> *Lord, You promise to give us wisdom if we ask, so we, Your humble servants, ask You for wisdom to rightly divide Your Word of truth. Guide us, Holy Spirit. Amen (James 1:5; 2 Tim. 2:15).*

Alright, here we go. I want us to look at this topic in three sections, but I think we'll leave the Neapolitan ice cream in the freezer for this one. Here's how we'll tackle this sobering subject:

1. What the Old Testament says about Hell

2. What Jesus says about Hell

3. What the Bible says about Hell at the end of time

1. What the Old Testament says about Hell

There is no mention of the word *Hell* in the Old Testament. As we discussed last week, the one word used to talk about the afterlife in the Old Testament is *Sheol*. This was said to be the destiny of all who died, both the wicked and the righteous. However, we noted there were hints in the Old Testament that though the wicked and righteous dead were both in Sheol, they were in different areas of this realm of the dead—as in two compartments. This seemed to be confirmed with Jesus's parable of the rich man and Lazarus (Luke 16:19-31), which we'll discuss more in a moment.

In the books written by the prophets, we do find hints of what was ultimately coming for those who rejected God.

> Read **Isaiah 66:24** and **Daniel 12:2**. What do these passages suggest about the Hebrew understanding of an afterlife for the unrighteous.

ISAIAH - WORMS, FIRE + THEY WILL
BE LOATHSOME

DANIEL - SHAME + EVERLASTING
CONTEMPT

Shame, everlasting contempt, unending worms, and perpetual fire awaited those who rebelled against the one true God. Painful, right?

> But lest we think God is a sadistic tyrant who takes pleasure in people's eternal demise, take a look at **Ezekiel 18:23,32; 33:11**. How do these verses show you the heart of God for people's souls?

23 - PLEASED WHEN THEY TURN FROM EVIL WAYS
32 - REPENT + LIVE
33:11 - TURN FROM EVIL WAYS

God repeatedly communicated through the prophet Ezekiel that He wanted the wicked to repent, turn to Him, and live, thus avoiding their eternal destruction. That sentiment continued to be expressed in the New Testament.

> Read **2 Peter 3:8-9**. How does this passage show that the heart of God has not and will not change?

HE is patient, He wants everyone to come to repentance

> How does that truth impact your relationship with God and other people?

Be patient + compassionate

Oh, my friend, I want to show the same patience to others that Jesus shows to me and reflect the compassionate heart of God. If He is not willing that any of us should perish, then I don't want to be willing either! May God use each of us to be part of His ministry of reconciliation (2 Cor. 5:18-19).

2. What Jesus says about Hell

> Read **John 15:9,13** and describe Jesus's nature and character.

9 - As He loves us, we should love each other - remain in His love
13 - Give all the love you can

Now, just sit for a second and ponder the truth that Jesus loves you like God loves Him. Kind of hard to grasp, isn't it? Jesus proved His love for you and me by giving His life for us on the cross. And this Jesus, our loving Savior, is full of grace and truth (John 1:14). Which means He will always give you grace and always tell you the truth. I want us to keep reading this day of study through the lens of Jesus's love, grace, and truth because, believe it or not, Jesus talked about Hell more than any person in Scripture. And what He had to say about it is not very pleasant.

What word for this afterlife location did Jesus use in **Luke 16:23** and **Matthew 11:23?**

Hell, down to the depths

Hades is the Greek word that best represents the Hebrew word we talked about last week— *Sheol*. In fact, in the Septuagint (LXX), which is the Greek translation of the Old Testament, *Hades* is used everywhere *Sheol* is used in the Hebrew text. So, like *Sheol*, *Hades* can refer simply to the realm of the dead. Yet, it can also be used to communicate the place where the unrighteous dead suffer when they die. In the parable in Luke 16, the rich man is said to be "in torment" and "in agony in this flame" (Luke 16:23-24). As we noted last week, we should be careful trying to build a doctrine on a parable. But "in this case Jesus' vivid description of the basic conditions of the godly and ungodly dead is indispensable to the parable's point."[3]

Like Sheol, though, Hades is not a dead end for the dead. It seems the unrighteous are destined for a different eternal existence.

Read the following passages and note the word Jesus used to speak of this place of punishment. (Watch for footnotes in your Bible that give the original Greek word.)

Matthew 5:22 Fire of Hell

Mark 9:43 Hell where the fire never goes out.

Luke 12:5 Hell

The word translated *Hell* in these texts and others throughout the Gospels is the Greek word *Gehenna*.[4]

What can you glean about the origin and nature of *Gehenna* from **2 Chronicles 28:3; Jeremiah 32:35?**

The word *Gehenna* is derived from the Hebrew phrase, *Ge Hinnom*, translated the *Valley of Hinnom*.[5] This valley is located just outside the gates of Jerusalem. As we learned from the texts, it had the heinous history of being the place of child sacrifice to the false god Molech. King Josiah stopped that atrocious practice, and tradition has it the valley became the place where sewage and trash were burned.

With this description, it makes sense that Jesus used *Gehenna* to describe Hell. But was Jesus using *Gehenna* as another name for the intermediate state of Hades or referring to a different place? Hmmm . . .

(Before we move on to our last section, you may need to procrastinate. Do you need to check your air conditioning filter, your text messages, or maybe water your plants? Procrastinating might make this hard subject a little easier to get through.)

3. What the Bible says about Hell at the end of time

When Christ returns, His followers will receive resurrection bodies and inhabit the new earth. This is our glorious unending.

But sadly, the unrighteous and unrepentant dead who inhabit Sheol/Hades transition also. They will have a not-so-glorious unending.

> How does **Revelation 20:11-15** reveal what happens to those who are in Hades?
>
> *They will be thrown in the lake of fire*

At the great white throne judgment, death and Hades will be thrown into the lake of fire. Some scholars believe the lake of fire is synonymous with *Gehenna*, the word Jesus used most often to talk about Hell. The Scripture says that not only will Hades be thrown into the lake of fire, but also the devil (19:20) and all those who have rejected Christ, those whose names are not found in the book of life (20:15).

This is some tough stuff, right? I've tried to pause during our study today to divert and distract with some playful procrastination, but oh, my sister, in all seriousness, my heart feels sick when I type those words. People in Hell will be disconnected from God forever, separated from Him. There are some who believe that those who enter eternity without

Christ will cease to exist. This belief is called *annihilationism*. The eternal fire of Hell remains, but those thrown into the lake of fire are consumed, no more, forever gone.

Based on the preponderance of Scripture, I think this interpretation is questionable. However, there are some details we will never know. We ask the Spirit to guide us into truth and enlighten our understanding.

> Read the sobering words of **2 Thessalonians 1:5-10**. What are the three things verse 9 says will happen to those who don't know God?

On that day of Christ's return, those who were in Hades will experience everlasting destruction, be shut out from the presence of the Lord, and separated from the glory of His power.

> How do those words hit you and how do you respond?

There are details we don't know about Hell, but what is undeniable is there will be no fellowship with God for those who have rejected Him.

My friend, that alone makes it Hell. To be cut off from the love, grace, and presence of Christ is unthinkable.

Even if the soul is annihilated and blotted out of existence, even that, compared to the joy of living forever in the comfort and love of God's presence, would be an appropriate definition of Hell.

Regardless, Hell is not funny or something to joke about. Hell is so serious that Jesus died to keep us from it. We will talk more about that tomorrow.

This day of study may have troubled you. Perhaps you're uncertain about your own future, or maybe someone you love died and you're concerned they may be experiencing this separation from God. Resist the urge to avoid or dismiss what is troubling you. Instead, call a Bible study buddy or another trusted Christian friend and pray about this. I certainly understand how difficult this truth is, and I am praying for you.

My friend, you can trust God's mercy for you and the ones you love. Remember the truth of Scripture: He is not willing that any of us should perish, but instead, that all of us should come to salvation (2 Pet. 3:9).

Last thing.

Take a deep breath and let these words of Paul wash over you as a blessing and comfort.

"Now may our Lord Jesus Christ Himself and God our Father, who has loved us and given us eternal comfort and good hope by grace, comfort and strengthen your hearts in every good work and word."

2 THESSALONIANS 2:16-17 (NASB)

Enough for today. Tomorrow some really good news! Whew!

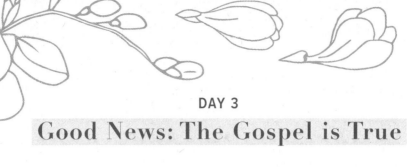

Good News: The Gospel is True

"The gospel is not a doctrine of the tongue, but of life. It cannot be grasped by reason and memory only, but it is fully understood when it possesses the whole soul and penetrates to the inner recesses of the heart."[6]

JOHN CALVIN

Oh my, aren't you so glad we are out of Hell? Yesterday was a hard day of study as we looked at the sad truth that Hell is real. And if not for the truth of today's study—that the gospel is true—we would all need to quit right now and eat a whole gallon of Neapolitan ice cream!

There would be no hope without the gospel and no need for Heaven without the gospel.

Today, we'll examine what the gospel actually is so we can follow the path God designed for us to spend eternity with Him. Pour your coffee or tea or ice-cold sparkling whatever you like, and let's pause and pray.

> *Lord, instruct us and teach us in the way we should go. Counsel us with Your loving eye on us. Amen (Ps. 32:8).*

Let's go back to where we started the study with the disciples' conversation with Jesus in John 14.

> Review Jesus's words in **John 14:1-4**. What question was asked in John 14:5, and who asked it?

Thomas — "Lord, We don't know where we are going, so how can we know the way?"

I love Thomas, don't you? He cuts right to it. *How can we know the way? We don't know enough. We don't even know where you are going. Uh, Jesus, could you be more specific?*

What a great setup for Jesus to answer clearly. Thanks, Thomas!

How did Jesus describe Himself and how we get to the Father in **John 14:6**?

No one gets to the Father except through Him.

The first two words Jesus used, "I am," have super significance. In fact, look that phrase up in your favorite Bible resource, or do an internet search for a phrase like "biblical meaning of I am." Jot down what you find that explains why those words are so important.

Jesus was claiming to be God by using the words, "I am," and proclaiming that He is the way to the Father's House.

Does this really mean Jesus is claiming there's only one way to salvation, to the Father, to Heaven? What do you think, and why?

Now, put down your pen for a moment. We're going for a drive.

My friend Angela and I were rolling down the highway when she struck up a conversation about her spiritual frustration. For several miles, she explained how she grew up in church, loved God, and believed in Jesus. But something was off. She was confused and conflicted because she only felt the coldness of religion, all the "thou shalt" and "thou shalt not," rather than the warmth and security of a relationship with God.

After she spouted all her doubts and angst, we pulled into the driveway, her hands still gripping the steering wheel. I turned to her from the passenger seat and asked, "Do you believe what Jesus said about Himself?" I went on to quote John 14:6 and told her that Jesus claimed to be the only way to the Father. He claimed to not just tell the truth, but to be the truth embodied. He didn't just say He would give life; He had the audacity to say He was life itself.

She sat quietly for a moment, then tears formed in the corners of her eyes. "I'm not sure I've ever really grasped that. Jesus was part of the way and lots of truth, but my church and legalism and my upbringing—all that seemed to yell more loudly that their way was the way, they were the truth, and if you didn't want to go to Hell, you better follow the rules, never miss a Sunday in church, not cuss, confess sins . . . ," and she began to laugh through her tears as her list went on and on.

So, cram yourself in the front seat with Angela and me for a moment. What would you say to my question? Do you believe what Jesus said about Himself? As you ponder that for a moment, consider that Jesus's words about Himself are the heartbeat of the gospel and the key that opens Heaven's door.

Let's look at the following Scriptures to identify the path to the Father based on what these verses teach. This may be very familiar to you, so protect yourself from "familiarity fatigue" by rephrasing each verse in your own words using first-person pronouns. This will remind you of the radical, personal implications of these claims. If this is new to you, use the same first-person method so you get the full implication of each holy word on your life and future. I've done the first one to get you started.

Romans 3:23 *I have sinned and fallen short of the glory of God.*

Romans 6:23 The gift, in eternal life is in Jesus

Ephesians 2:8

John 3:18 Believe in God or be condemned

John 3:16 God gave His son to save us

Romans 5:8 Christ died to save us

Acts 4:12 Salvation is found only in Jesus

Romans 10:9-10

Now read your list of responses out loud, in order, as one seamless thought.

What are your thoughts as you process what you just read aloud?

What response do you need to make to what you read?

Oh, my friend, you just read the gospel—the good news! And that good news is for you and for the whole world. We don't embrace Christ simply to avoid Hell; we respond to Christ because His love draws us and His grace compels us. His forgiveness cleans us, and His Spirit secures and sustains us.

He is the truth. To refuse Christ is to accept a lie. He is the Way. To reject Christ is to invite a wandering path. He is the Life. To renounce Him is to embrace death.

I encourage you to finish up this day in one of two ways. If you have already trusted Christ as your Savior, center your thoughts, praise, and gratefulness on that truth. Think back to your life before Christ and how the gospel has changed and enriched your life. Journal your thoughts, pray over them, and share them with somebody.

Take a pic of the personalized verses you wrote (from Rom. 3:23 to Rom. 10:9-10) and post them to social media. What a great way to show what Jesus has done for you. Don't forget to tag me and use #HeavenStudy so I can celebrate with you!

If you have not trusted in Christ and Christ alone to be your Savior and Lord (like my friend Angela), do it right now! Call on Him. He is as close as your breath. He is listening for your sincere heart call and confession. He will save you right now. Call a Bible study buddy or another trusted Christian friend and tell them about your decision. Ask them to pray for you and with you and help you understand next steps in following Christ.

> "Now this is eternal life: that they know you, the only true God, and Jesus Christ, whom you have sent."

> **JOHN 17:3**

I hope this day of study, centered on the gospel, drew you to deeper appreciation, adoration, or acceptance of the true treasure of Heaven: Jesus.

To Him be all praise.

And all the sisters said, Amen!!!

DAY 4

Eternal Rewards

"That is why, at the end of all things, when the sun rises here and the twilight turns to blackness down there, the blessed will say, "we have never lived anywhere except in Heaven."[7]

C. S. LEWIS

If we're new friends, you may not know that I love, well, am kind of obsessed with, dead authors! My very favorite forever and always is C. S. Lewis. But he's not the only one. There is just something about the way those old writers used language that thrills and comforts and challenges me. I am a big fan!

So, I have to tell you what I found in Rachel Field's 1938 novel, *All This and Heaven Too*. Field notes at the beginning of her book that the title is accredited to Matthew Henry, who also happens to be one of my favorite dead authors! If you don't know Matt (yeah, I treat him like we're old friends), he was a British minister and author in the late 1600s–early 1700s. He is probably best known for his complete six-volume commentary on the Bible. (Which, by the way, is sitting on my shelf right now because I inherited the set from my dad.) Anyway, Henry wrote of his father, the Reverend Philip Henry, "He would say sometimes when he was in the midst of the comforts of this life, 'All this, and Heaven too!'"[8]

Perhaps you've heard that phrase? "All this and Heaven too." I love that Matthew Henry's dad said that when life was at its best. *Like, all this blessing and still there is more? Heaven? Wow!*

I need that perspective as I think of eternal rewards. You may too. Let's ask God to align our hearts with His Word.

> *Lord, help us to consider clearly and accurately our priceless privilege of knowing You, and may we see everything else through that lens today. Amen (Phil. 3:8-9).*

Gotta be honest here, the thought of getting rewards in Heaven feels superfluous to me and a bit awkward. Isn't knowing Christ here on earth and being with Him forever reward enough?

Study your heart before we study Scripture. What are your thoughts on eternal rewards? Isn't Jesus reward enough?

Why do you think our works merit reward when our righteousness is in Christ, not works?

Don't worry if you aren't sure about all this. The Bible is, so turn to **1 Corinthians 15:58** and **Hebrews 6:10** and write down how God sees your works.

You can give yourself one hundred percent to the work of the Lord because your labor is not in vain. It is not meaningless. It matters, and God never overlooks it.

Now read **Romans 14:10-12** and **2 Corinthians 5:10** and describe the event that's mentioned and what will take place at this event.

All believers will show up at the judgment seat of Christ upon His return to give an account of how we've lived our lives.

Before we go any further, let's get clear on some things.

Three Important Truths About the Judgment Seat of Christ

1. This is not a judgment of your salvation. That decision was already made and sealed when you were born again. (See John 5:24; Rom. 8:1; 1 John 2:2.)

2. This is not a judgment of your sin. You are no longer held eternally accountable for your sin when you are in Christ. (See 2 Cor. 5:17; Col. 3:9–10; and 1 John 1:9.)

3. This occurs when Christ returns and ushers in the new heaven and new earth. (See Rev. 22:12.) (We'll learn more about this in Session Five.)

At this judgment seat, Christ will reward us accordingly for how we've lived our lives. Now, the word *judgment* can stir up all sorts of insecurity, intimidation, and resistance because it sounds so, well, judgy! But let's get some context to help us understand the judgment seat of Christ the way the first-century Christians would have.

In Greek, the word translated *judgment seat* is *bema*. A *bema* was actually a raised platform on which an athletic judge sat to observe an athlete during a game.[9] The one on the *bema* wasn't judging if the player was an athlete. He wasn't judging if the athlete had skill or was qualified to play. He was there to acknowledge how the athlete played and reward him accordingly. The judgment seat of Christ will be similar. As one scholar put it: "The judgment pronounced is not a declaration of doom, but an *assessment of worth*, with the assignment of rewards to those who because of their faithfulness deserve them, and the *loss* or withholding of rewards in the case of those who do not deserve them.[10]

If you are in Christ, you will someday stand before that *bema*, that judgment seat.

How does knowing this judgment is coming hit you? Are you intimidated? Joyful? Still processing? Motivated to work harder? Fearful of Jesus's disapproval?

Honestly study your heart on this and jot down your thoughts and emotions.

You may have mixed emotions and conflicted thoughts about this, so let's pause and consider who will be on that *bema*. Christ, the One spoken of in Romans 5:8, will look on us with love—a love He demonstrated to us while we were hopeless in our sin.

He will look at us with that same love when we stand before Him as His beloved bride. He won't judge our sin because He already received that judgment for us. He isn't going to be angry that we never conquered our sin completely. He understands what it is like to be tempted.

The same love that compelled Christ to die for us is the same love that will radiate from the *bema* on that day. So don't let Satan hijack this truth and use it to frighten you or turn you away from Christ. Let the Spirit of Christ work within you to accomplish what brings Him glory (Phil. 2:13). Let the love of Christ draw you to lovingly serve Him.

Labor out of love, my friend, not legalism or fear (Ps. 100:1-3; 1 John 4:18).

Pour yourself some coffee or tea and take a little break to think and pray about what you have experienced so far today. I know I need to. I don't want to dread appearing before Christ's judgment seat. I want to feel safe there. And I will be, and so will you, because our lives are hidden in Christ and covered in His righteousness.

Now, let's leave the place of accountability and reward to determine the type of reward we might be given.

The word *reward* in Greek is *misthos* (Matt. 5:12). It's a word also used to communicate wage or payment (Matt. 20:8; 1 Tim. 5:18).

> But look at **Acts 1:18** and jot down how *misthos* is used to describe the fruit of Judas's choice.

Sorry for the graphic scene, but you get the idea. *Misthos* is the result or the earned fruition of an action.

And we are promised the joy of eternal *misthos*! So what form does the reward come in?

FIVE CROWNS

Of course, the greatest reward for us in Heaven will be seeing and being with Christ for eternity. However, the Bible does speak of five crowns we will receive for our faithful service.

> Look up the following passages and jot down what you find out about each crown and what it represents.
>
> **1 Corinthians 9:25**
>
> **1 Thessalonians 2:19**
>
> **2 Timothy 4:8**
>
> **James 1:12**
>
> **1 Peter 5:4**

That's a lot of crowns for one puny head!

The *crown* mentioned in these passages is best understood as a laurel wreath placed around the head of a victorious athlete to reward his success.

When speaking of these crowns, Justin Taylor writes, "Though it is popular to see these as different types of reward . . . a majority of commentators believe these are different ways of referring to the one reward of eternal life."[11]

Taylor also notes that there could be varying degrees of rewards given in the form of greater capacity or responsibilities.

Regardless of which view taken, the Bible does speak of rewards and/or crowns for the faithful Christ follower. My response to that: Wow! I'm blown away that God planned that for us. After all, He didn't have to. But here is where I land on this. Whether it is one reward or five crowns or a virtual shelf of trophies, the main thing is not what we get someday; it is what we already have on this day.

We have Christ and the privilege of knowing Him.

Look at how Paul laid this out in **Philippians 3:7-9**. Summarize his main point.

Before Paul says that nothing compares to the surpassing excellence of knowing Christ, read what he listed as successes in **Philippians 3:4-6**.

He called all these successes loss. In and of themselves, they were good things, but nothing, absolutely nothing, compares to the reward of knowing Christ. There is no greater satisfaction, and there is salvation in no other name.

Oh, my friend, could there ever be any reward that compares to the ultimate reward of knowing Jesus in this life and in the life to come?

Pause and write a prayer, pouring your heart out to Jesus.

Dear Lord,

Amen

If our ultimate reward is Christ and we will be rewarded in Heaven for our life in Him, how should we respond here on earth based on the following verses?

Matthew 5:12

Luke 6:23

Rejoice! Leap for joy! Be glad! Wow. That is quite the emotional outburst, isn't it?

Jesus suggests we express all that emotion because of our imminent and ultimate reward!

So, if you are having a bad day, think about that coming day, the day you will receive a reward you never deserved because Christ took the wages of your sin that He didn't deserve. Yep, all that and Heaven too!

I love You, Lord. Thank You for Your faithfulness to us. May You find us faithful too. Amen.

All right, Session Two is a wrap! Flip back to page 19, review your "Troubled Heart List," and consider how what you're learning is impacting what you wrote.

Tomorrow, check out our *Takeaway Truths* and then enjoy your *Dash Living Day*.

And here's a teaser: We're going to share a plum and a prune in the next video teaching. You'll love it; you'll see!

TAKEAWAY TRUTHS

Below are some important points we covered this week. There's also room for you to add other takeaways you want to remember.

- Regardless of religion or culture, the prevalent thought among most people is that there is something more beyond this life. The reason: God has put eternity in our hearts.

- Life is short, and every person has an appointment with death.

- Hell is a real place where the unrighteous will be forever separated from God. Different words are used for Hell in Scripture, including Hades, Gehenna, and the lake of fire. The New Testament seems to speak of the unrighteous dead currently being in Hades, but at the final judgment they will be condemned to the lake of fire.

- Our hope for Heaven is found only in the gospel—repenting of our sins and placing our faith in Christ.

- All followers of Christ will stand before the judgment seat of Christ (*bema* seat) to give an account of how they've lived. The judgment seat of Christ is not about salvation or condemnation but about rewards for our work for Christ. Exactly what the rewards will be is unknown.

HOW YOU WANT TO BE REMEMBERED

Losing a loved one can be hard—whether a grandparent or sibling or child or friend. What makes it hard is also the most treasured thing we can hang on to: our memories of them.

What about you? How do you want to be remembered? Thinking about how we want to be remembered, whether by someone we only know for a brief moment now or by our loved ones when we move on to our eternal home can impact how we live now—in the dash. It can reduce some of the emotional clutter that complicates our sense of priority and help keep us focused on our purpose.

> On the tombstone below, write one sentence about who you are, what you value, and how you want to be remembered. Maybe it's a Bible verse, a favorite quote, song lyric, or just a statement you compose. But think about it. How would you want your life to be summarized? This sentence can be used as an epitaph, or commemorative statement, representing your life. You may want to write it in pencil for now because you're still in process. Your statement may change as you grow and change.

"Teach us to number our days, that we may gain a heart of wisdom."

PSALM 90:12

NUMBERING OUR DAYS

HEBREWS 9:27

BEFORE THE VIDEO

Welcome and Prayer

Psalm 90
2 Cor 5:11

WATCH THE VIDEO

THREE PRINCIPLES AND ONE PRAYER FROM PSALM 90:

1. **Admit our** *frailty*

PROV 31:35

  • Rebrand your frailty as *strength* and *dignity*.

Psalm 139 13-16

2. **Acknowledge life's** *brevity*.

  • Rebrand every *tombstone* as a *stepping* stone.

3. **Ask God for** *clarity*.

LUKE 6:23

  • Time is not a *commodity*. It's something we *steward*.

  • Prayer: Psalm 90:17

ECC 13:11

  • Rebrand every day as a slice of *eternity*.

MATT 25 14-28

THREE Ls:

1. *LAUGH*

2. *LEAP*

3. *LOOK*

Go to **jenniferrothschild.com** to get a summary of this video teaching in your inbox. And you'll find there a *Heaven* playlist to keep your heart tilted toward *Heaven*.

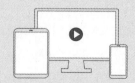

To access the video teaching sessions, use the instructions in the back of your Bible study book.

CONVERSATION GUIDE

PERSONAL BIBLE STUDY

- What was your favorite day of study? Why?

- What does it mean that you were made for eternity? Why is it important we keep that in mind?

- As believers in Christ, what should be our response to what we learn about Hell?

- Why is Jesus the only way to the Father? How is this claim the heart of the gospel?

- How do you answer people who say Jesus's claim is too exclusive and not fair?

- Our works merit reward, but our righteousness is found only in Christ. How does that work?

- Which *Takeaway Truth* stands out to you and why?

- *Dash Living Day*: What did you write on the tombstone and why?

VIDEO TEACHING

- What's one thing that stood out to you from the video teaching? Why?

- How does admitting our frailty better help us live for eternity?

- Jennifer said "Eden had no tombstones." What's the significance of that statement, especially in light of the brevity of life?

- How can we see tombstones as stepping stones?

- What does it mean to number our days, and why is that significant in living our Christian lives the way we should?

- Are you being a good steward of the time on earth you've been given? If so, how? If not, what changes do you need to make?

SESSION THREE

"But Christ has indeed been raised from the dead, the firstfruits of those who have fallen asleep. For since death came through a man, the resurrection of the dead comes also through a man. For as in Adam all die, so in Christ all will be made alive."

1 CORINTHIANS 15:20-22

YOU
WILL
RISE

If Christ had not risen, we would have no hope for our own resurrection. Grasping the significance of Christ's resurrection is pivotal to understanding our eternal future in Heaven.

In this week of study, we'll dive into 1 Corinthians 15. Examining this chapter will help us understand the nature of Christ's resurrection, how His resurrection guarantees our resurrection, the nature of our resurrected bodies, and our ultimate victory over death. Get set to raise a hallelujah this week!

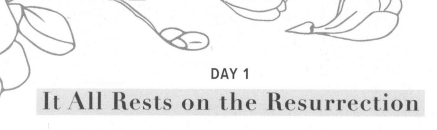

DAY 1

It All Rests on the Resurrection

"The New Testament writers speak as if Christ's achievement in rising from the dead was the first event of its kind in the whole history of the universe."[1]

C. S. LEWIS

Well, my friend, we have made it to Session Three! I'm so grateful you are sticking with me. I wonder how much of your loyalty has to do with the Neapolitan ice cream? Kidding.

Today I want to start with water. Yep, pour a plain glass of water. I've got mine sitting here on my white glass-top desk. I chose to pour my water into a delicately etched piece of stemware I got at a wedding reception as a party favor.

I love sipping from its thin rim. I like to wrap my fingertips around its graceful stem and palm the globe to imagine the engraving. It makes me feel so fancy! And I just love how the tinkle of the ice sounds like wind chimes when I tilt it toward my lips.

So grab a glass of water. And if it matters to you, choose a glass that brings you a smile. Go ahead. I'll wait.

Now, think back to your middle school science class. Do you remember what the chemical composition of water is?

Yes, H_2O! The girl's still got it!

What do the H and the O stand for?
___HYDROGEN___ and ___OXYGEN___

Look into your water and imagine this: invisible to your eye, but very present, are gazillions and bazillions (I have no idea how many) of H_2O molecules.

Now imagine you're a highly intelligent and very attractive rockstar chemist and you have all the best equipment to remove the oxygen atoms from the H_2O molecules.

What would you have left after you successfully removed all the oxygen?

Yep, you'd be left with only hydrogen atoms (H).

But if you did that, you would no longer have water. Water (H_2O) cannot exist without oxygen atoms (O). I hope you aren't a thirsty chemist.

Why did I start with a sip of water and an amateur chemistry refresher? Because this illustration applies to the resurrection and eternal life. Whaaat?

You'll see. Let's pray first.

Jesus, we put our faith in You. Thank You for giving us Your Spirit. Let the river of Living Water flow through us as we study Your Word today. Amen (John 7:37-38).

Go to **1 Corinthians 15**. Put down your pen. Don't take notes or underline; just sip your water while you read all 58 verses. Ask the Holy Spirit to bring His Word to life for you because we'll be in this chapter all week. Take as much time as you need. You can also do what I do— listen to it. (My favorite way to listen is with the *Dwell* Bible app.) If you listen, it will take you about nine minutes.

Now, pick up your pen. Even though you were just reading or listening to get familiar with the text, journal your impressions or thoughts about what you experienced. What themes stuck out to you?

If this passage is new or confusing to you, don't let that trouble your heart. We will take it slow and simple because, well, slow and simple is how I roll when it comes to potentially complex concepts.

Look at **verses 1–5**. What four things did Paul say were of first importance?

1. CHRIST DIED FOR OUR SINS
2. HE WAS BURIED
3. HE WAS RAISED ON THE 3rd day
4. HE APPEARED TO THE DISCIPLES

It is of first importance that Christ died for our sins and was raised from the dead, not according to our religious tradition, not according to superstition or wishful thinking, but according to the Scripture (1 Thess. 2:13). The second and fourth statements reinforce the statements before them. That Christ was buried points to the reality of His death. That He appeared points to the reality of the resurrection.[2] These statements are the gospel in a nutshell. And of course, because the gospel is true, we want to receive it, hold fast to it, and stand firm in it.

Sometimes when we think of the gospel, we focus on the cross, the place Jesus bore and paid for our sins. But Paul was making a big deal about what followed Jesus's death—His resurrection.

Read **verses 12 and 13**. What was Paul's big idea, and how does it impact Heaven for us?

If there is no resurrection of the dead, then Christ is not risen. And if Christ has not risen, well, then you and I can't and won't be either.

It's interesting that the Corinthians believed Jesus was resurrected from the dead. What tripped them up, though, was their own resurrection from the dead. They were influenced by other thinking of the day. The Sadducees, for example, taught that anything past this life was just wishful thinking. The Greek philosophers taught resurrection was undesirable because a state of pure spirit was the highest form of being, not an updated, renovated body.[3]

The result of such influence? The Corinthian Christians believed they would live forever, but not in resurrected bodies.

So, what is the problem with this, and why does it really matter? Paul explained.

Read the verses below from **1 Corinthians 15** and write all the if/then implications of no resurrection.

Verse 13 If _there was no resurrection_, then _CHRIST has not been raised._

Verse 14 If _CHRIST HASN'T BEEN RAISED_, then _our teaching is useless_ and then _so is your faith_

Verse 16 If _the dead are not raised_, then _CHRIST has not been raised either._

Verse 17 If _CHRIST has not been raised_, then _your faith is futile_ and then _you are still in your sins will be lost_

Verse 18 And then _those who have fallen asleep_

Verse 19 If _we have hope in CHRIST_, then _we are pitied more than all men._

If there is no resurrection, then not even Christ has been raised. If Christ was not raised, our message and our faith is useless, and we are still in our sins. That means all those who died are forever lost.

And it's plain sad if we place our faith in Christ for this life only. That is something to be pitied, not celebrated.

Oh, my friend, the implications are huge if we deny that our resurrection is possible. It IS more than possible. Because of Jesus, it is guaranteed. Because He was resurrected, we will be resurrected. His guarantees ours.

Martin Luther wrote, "Everything depends on our retaining a firm hold on this doctrine in particular; for if this one totters and no longer counts, all the others will lose their value and validity."[4]

Our hope of Heaven rests on the resurrection.

This day of study may have been heady for you. There were a few times I had to listen to the verses from 1 Corinthians 15 over and over to make sure I got all Paul's "if/thens"! So, if it took you a minute to absorb this, that's okay; we're all learning and growing together.

To close the day, pick up your glass of water again and imagine all those H_2O molecules. Remember how you pretended you were a highly intelligent and very attractive chemist who removed the oxygen atoms from the H_2O molecules? Remember the result? You only had hydrogen left. And without that combination of hydrogen and oxygen, you didn't have water. Removing the oxygen left you high and dry!

Well, if eternal life is water, then the death of Jesus is the hydrogen atom and the resurrection of Jesus is the oxygen atom. In other words, without His resurrection, our resurrection and eternal life itself would not exist. Jesus's death is essential, for His death was the payment for our sin and the satisfaction of God's wrath toward sin. Yet, if the gospel story ended there, death would have been more powerful than Jesus. And if death were more powerful than Jesus, then He wasn't God. The story would have ended there, as would our hope. But Jesus arose from the grave.

And because He arose, we will also rise to a glorious unending!

It all rests on the resurrection.

Take another sip of water and use the following verses, in the order listed, to create a prayer of affirmation, receiving, and thanking God for our eternal life.

Revelation 22:17; Isaiah 55:1; John 7:37–38

Where are you studying *Heaven* today? Post a picture on social media with your *Heaven* Bible study and glass of water. Don't forget to tag me and use #HeavenStudy.

Dear God,

WATER OF LIFE
FREE NOURISHMENT

We hear You call, Lord, and we come. We are thirsty, and we receive the free gift of the water of life.

Thank You for inviting us to drink and making living water flow from us because You have placed it in us.

Amen

Well, my glass is empty and my heart (and bladder) is full. Swallow those last few sips, and be reminded that He is good. See you tomorrow!

And by the way, if you actually are a highly intelligent and very attractive rockstar chemist, please forgive my wobbly analogy. I barely made it out of middle school science!

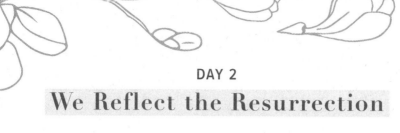

DAY 2

We Reflect the Resurrection

"He is the 'first fruits,' the 'pioneer of life.' He has forced open a door that has been locked since the death of the first man."[5]

C. S. LEWIS

Pour your coffee or tea (or maybe you're still sipping from your new favorite water glass from yesterday), settle in, and let me take you through some branches of my family tree, figuratively and literally.

There's a lush, beautiful fig tree growing in my brother David's Florida backyard, yet that tree started with our dad's grandmother. I never knew her, but Hero Dad told lots of stories about his "Mama" who lived in Stone Mountain, Georgia.

When Mama's sister Lucy moved from Stone Mountain to Ocoee, Florida, in the 1920s, Lucy took a piece of Mama's fig tree and rooted it in her new Florida backyard.

Then my dad's parents, who I called Mama and Papa, brought a piece of Great Aunt Lucy's fig tree back to Clearwater for my parents to plant in our backyard. It rooted and grew large outside our garage door there on Albright Drive.

Around that time, my mom's parents moved from Clearwater up to the panhandle of Florida, and my granddaddy took a piece of that fig tree and planted it by the Apalachicola River. It grew and produced enough figs that my grandmother, who we affectionately called Sarah Burg, made fig preserves every summer.

When Granddaddy died and Sarah Burg sold the house, my mom went back to the river one last time to break off a branch of that fig tree to plant in their latest home in Pensacola. Then, when my parents moved from Pensacola over a decade later, of course, she broke off a couple of small branches of that tree to root in the backyard where she lives now in central Florida.

Her fig tree is large and healthy and is bursting with wonderful sun-kissed figs every summer. My mom rooted a piece for my brother David, and it's flourishing in his backyard now on the west coast of Florida.

The legacy of that one tree from Mama's Georgia backyard has spanned over one hundred years and spawned four generations of happy little trees (as Bob Ross would say).

It has nourished and beautified at least seven different homes over the decades. My mom calls it the "heritage fig," and rightly so!

That fig tree in my mom's backyard is the one I talked about in my *Amos* Bible study. So, if you did that Bible Study with me, you have enjoyed what Mama started too!

Now that you're all tangled up in the limbs of my family's horticultural history (and perhaps craving a Fig Newton®—sorry), read **1 Corinthians 15:20-23** (CSB) below and (circle) what Jesus is called when it comes to our resurrection.

> "But as it is, Christ has been raised from the dead, the firstfruits of those who have fallen asleep. For since death came through a man, the resurrection of the dead also comes through a man. For just as in Adam all die, so also in Christ all will be made alive. But each in his own order: Christ, the firstfruits; afterward, at his coming, those who belong to Christ."

Before we study this together, let's ask God to guide us in His Word.

Teach us Your ways, Lord, that we may walk in Your truth. Amen (Ps. 86:11).

What does it mean that Christ was the firstfruits? Where does that thought or term come from? Let's do some digging in the Old Testament to find out.

Leviticus 23 contains information on the different feasts that the Israelites were to celebrate. Verses 9-14 deal specifically with the Feast of Firstfruits. Describe in general what took place at this feast.

The Israelites brought the very first sheaf of their grain harvest as a sacrifice to the Lord. There is debate over when this festival was to take place. In this passage, the timing is just a general "when you enter the land." However, there are hints in Exodus (23:14-16; 34:18-20) that this feast was to take place in the midst of the Passover celebration. The feast celebrated the goodness of God and acknowledged that He had provided the harvest. The firstfruits also signified that more of the harvest was to come. This was the first of the harvest. The rest of the crop was yet to be realized.

So, what Paul was saying in 1 Corinthians 15:20-23 is that Christ, as firstfruits, is a representative of what's to come. One scholar says it like this: "Christ is the first to be raised from the dead and representative of more resurrection bodies to come. The metaphor of firstfruits functions similarly to the metaphor of a down payment or a pledge."[6]

> Now read **Matthew 28:1-10** and describe how this passage connects to the Leviticus passage.

It was in the midst of the Passover celebration, on the first day after the Sabbath, that Jesus rose from the dead. Yes! Firstfruit! The picture of what was to come!

> Oh, but wait . . . Let's think about this for a moment. Was Jesus really the first one in the Bible to come back to life after He died? What other examples do we have in Scripture of a dead person being brought back to life? (Hint: See **1 Kings 17:17-24**; **Luke 7:11-17**; **John 11:38-44.**) Describe the who and what of these examples and what makes them different from Jesus's resurrection.

The child, the widow's son, and Lazarus were revived and resuscitated, but they were not resurrected. They came back to life in their same mortal, decaying bodies. Eventually, they physically died again.

Jesus was resurrected to a new glorious body, never to die again. Death was conquered.

We will also have a resurrection body that won't die. That may make you wonder what these new bodies will be like. Well, if you wonder about that, you are in good company.

> Read **1 Corinthians 15:35** and jot down the two questions that were raised to Paul.
>
> How are the dead raised
> What kind of body will they have

> Paul answered the second question in upcoming verses. But he didn't really answer the first one. Why do you think not?

> Look at **Acts 26:8** to see how Paul dealt with Agrippa on this same question.

"Why should any of you consider it incredible that God raises the dead?"

Uh, Paul, because it is incredible! But the principle is that nothing, even the incredible, is impossible for God (Luke 1:37). So why bother asking the "how" when we know the "who," right? Amen and amen.

But on to that second question.

> How does **Philippians 3:20-21** clue you into what kind of body you will have?

We will be conformed to Jesus's glorious body.

Tomorrow we'll see what your resurrected body may be like, but for now, don't think *compare*, think *conform*. In other words, don't try to compare your real body on earth to your ideal body on earth. That is far too limiting. Rather, think of your body being conformed to Jesus's risen body. That is mind-blowing!

> Read **1 Corinthians 15:36-38**.

How do these verses encourage you to think of your earthly body when it dies?

☑ As a seed
☐ As an early version of your later body
☐ As a corpse

Our bodies are like a seed that will be buried and eventually raised to life.

When my great grandmother planted a fig seed over one hundred years ago, she didn't expect a bigger fig seed to be the result. Of course not! When you sow any kind of seed, you don't expect a bigger, more bloated, exaggerated version of that seed to eventually break through the soil. You expect that seed to die as it is sown, and in its death to be transformed.

So, my friend, when you and I die, when our bodies are "planted" in the ground, what will rise when Christ returns will not be that same exact body in the version it was sown. That body is not fit for Heaven. We have to have a new one. That may help answer a question you might have about bodies that, for whatever reason, are not buried. If you know Christ, you don't have to have a fully formed body in the ground to receive a new one when Christ returns. You won't swap out the old one for a new one. You will immediately receive your new resurrection body, regardless of what state the old one is in.

So death is not an ending but a sowing.

Our resurrected bodies will reflect our Savior's glorified risen body. We will see Him and be like Him.

Oh, how sweet it is!

> Write out **Job 19:25-27** as a prayer and pray it all day, thanking God that your resurrection is secure and you will see Him someday!

MY REDEEMER LIVES

Good job; you're done for today! See you tomorrow.

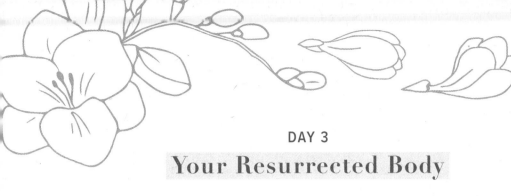

Your Resurrected Body

"The best moment of a Christian's life is his last one, because it is the one which is nearest heaven; and then it is that he begins to strike the key-note of the song which he shall sing to all eternity."[7]

CHARLES SPURGEON

I'll start with a confession: I have way too many denim jackets. (Okay, eleven. Is that too many?) Don't judge. I'm actually wearing one right now as I type this. I own several colors and styles—blue, blush, embroidered, distressed, blingy, gray, black, tailored, boxy, white, and even a yellow one! Yes, I may have a problem.

But that isn't my point.

I have one denim jacket I want to tell you about. It's a medium denim blue with silver buttons, and I got it at Gap® in 1999. It is that old! I have worn it on hundreds of grocery runs, on airplanes, holding toddlers, sitting in middle school gyms, flying to foreign countries, and even on video shoots. There have been years, depending on my weight, when it was a little snug, and other years when it was a bit too roomy. But it always seems to fit and never gets old! I have a feeling it will outlive me. Girl, it is like when I put it on, I am putting on the imperishable!

Do you have any piece of clothing like that? If so, just for fun, describe it.

If not, congratulations. You are likely very stylish. (And for sure you are not a hoarder!)

Well, whether you own a seemingly imperishable piece of clothing or not, because of Christ's resurrection, one day you will be clothed with the literal imperishable. Let's get a glimpse of what that heavenly wardrobe will be like.

But first, pause and pray, then review.

Lord, anchor our souls in the hope You give. Make us firm and secure in our High Priest, our Savior Jesus. Teach us truth today. Amen (Heb. 6:19-20).

Before we talk about the imperishable, look back at page 24 to review your Neapolitan ice cream timeline again. What we've been talking about this week in 1 Corinthians 15 takes place in the strawberry flavor—the time from Christ's return to forever. But let's revisit the vanilla flavor—the time between Christ's resurrection and His return, to make sure this is clear in our heads.

If you die before Christ's return, your final remains (in whatever form your body may be) will be left here on earth while your soul will be fully alive in the presence of God.

Your soul or your spirit?

I need us to pull over here for a minute and talk about your soul. Or is it your spirit? Are they the same thing? Or are they two different things? Are we body, soul, and spirit? Or just body and spirit/soul? Theologians have discussed this for hundreds of years and are yet to reach consensus. So, if they haven't figured this out in centuries, we won't try to do so in a paragraph. But here are three views on the issue; most people land on one of these three.

1. Genesis 2:7 tells us that God created man a living soul. Some interpret this to mean that the union of our body and spirit make up a human soul. This is interesting to me because when I fly, I often hear the flight attendants count the people on the plane and then report that there are one hundred and fifty eight "souls" on board.

2. Some believe that when the Bible speaks of soul and spirit, they are talking about the same things. They see the words as synonymous and can be used interchangeably (Luke 1:46-47; Isa. 26:9).

3. Lastly, some conclude through their understanding of Scripture that each human consists of three distinct parts—body, soul, and spirit (1 Thess. 5:23; Heb. 4:12).

Where you land on this is not essential to your faith. What matters is that you seek God and trust that what Genesis 1:27 and Psalm 139 say is true about all humans: we are fearfully and wonderfully made in His image. In Him we find our worth and value.

For the purposes of this Bible study, we are going to simplify our communication and use the words soul and spirit interchangeably.

Now, back to your regularly scheduled Bible study . . .

Turn to **Luke 23:46.**

What did Jesus say to God in those final moments as He hung on the cross?

What happened after Jesus committed His spirit to God?

What does His prayer indicate about what happens when we die?

At the moment of Jesus's last breath here on earth, at the moment His physical heart beat its last, Jesus's spirit was immediately in God's presence. Jesus's dead body was taken off the cross and buried, yet Jesus's spirit was fully alive.

When our bodies die, just like when Jesus's body died, they will not have any life hidden in them.

How did Paul describe those who died in Christ in **1 Thessalonians 4:13-14** and **1 Corinthians 15:6,51?**

FALL ASLEEP | Be Changed

If there's no life left in the body when it dies, why do you think *sleep* was used to describe death?

According to Scripture, Jesus's soul was not asleep upon His bodily death, and neither will ours be upon our deaths. We won't be in some kind of unaware rest until our bodies are animated on Christ's return.

When the biblical writers used sleep to speak of death, they were being metaphorical, not literal. Just think of that old hymn by Martin Luther, "A Mighty Fortress is Our God." Luther used a metaphor to describe God. God is not literally a giant impenetrable garrison made of ancient stone surrounded by watchtowers and turrets. The metaphor is used to communicate that God is strong, safe, and powerful.

The same applies to the biblical writer's use of the word *sleep*. It is a metaphor indicating that death is not the period at the end of the sentence; it is merely a comma.

Oh, my friend, someday we will all die. Yet, in the context of our eternal life, it is like our bodies will merely be sleeping until they are awakened to resurrection life at Christ's return. It is like the seed of our body is sown and germinates in the grave until it blossoms forth in resurrected life all at once, in a moment. In the twinkling of an eye, we will be clothed with our resurrection bodies.

And oh, what a wardrobe it will be!

In the following verses from **1 Corinthians 15**, note how Paul points out the contrasts between the body that is buried and how it will be clothed when we are raised to resurrection life.

Verse 42   Sown PERISHABLE

Raised IMPERISHABLE

Verse 43   Sown DISHONOR

Raised GLORY

Sown WEAKNESS

Raised POWER

Verse 44 Sown _NATURAL BODY_

Raised _SPIRITUAL BODY_

The natural body that was subject to sin and suffering, that grew weary and wasted away, will be raised a spiritually incorruptible body ready to inhabit the new earth, our forever Heaven.

Let's check out a few features of these resurrected bodies.

1. YOUR RESURRECTED BODY WILL BE INCORRUPTIBLE AND IMMORTAL.

First, read **1 Corinthians 15:51-53** and describe the when, what, and how of this heavenly wardrobe update.

Calling this a mystery is a bit of an understatement, if you ask me. It's difficult to wrap our earth-bound brains around how we will all be changed in a moment when Christ returns—when we trade our corruptible bodies for incorruptible ones, mortal bodies for immortal ones.

This is such a big deal that we need to pull over and ponder these words. Write a dictionary definition of the following.

Corruptible _Immoral or dishonest_

Incorruptible _Not susceptile to corruption_

Mortal _A living being, subject to death_

Immortal _Living forever, never dying or decaying_

Review the definitions you just wrote. Use them to describe your life now, then to describe your risen life forever.

How can the truth about your immortality and incorruptibility inform your experience today in a mortal and corruptible body?

We will not decay or die. We will no longer be subject to sin or suffering. I won't be blind. You won't fight depression. Your loved one won't have cancer. We will be like our risen Christ—our bodies conformed to His resurrected body.

Flip over to **Psalm 16:10** and read how Jesus's immortality and incorruptible nature was described thousands of years before He walked our soil.

God will not Forget us when we die

Beautiful, right? God's faithful One, Christ, never saw decay.

And you and me? Because we are found in Him, our resurrected bodies will not see decay either! You may need to break out in some major praise about now. I do!

2. YOUR RESURRECTED BODY WILL BE SPIRITUAL.

Read **John 20:5-7**. How did Peter find Jesus's grave cloths?

Strips of linen Head covering

The seemingly undisturbed linen cloths and the folded head covering describe a neat and tidy tomb. The Greek wording in this passage is interesting. When it says Simon Peter "saw the strips of linen," the word for *saw* doesn't mean a casual glance but rather an interested look, a careful observation.[8] In our vernacular, we might say Peter saw something strange or weird about the clothes. The implication is that, unlike Lazarus, who needed help being unwrapped from his grave cloths, Jesus moved through His without a wrinkle remaining.

Now read **Luke 24:41-43; John 20:19,26-27**. What do those verses indicate about Jesus's resurrected body?

Want to listen in on a great conversation I had on Heaven? Go to **413Podcast.com/HeavenIsReal** to hear Lee Strobel give a compelling and comforting case for Heaven.

Luke's account shows that Jesus ate in His resurrected body (YES! And all the foodies said "Amen!") And John was quick to point out that Jesus showed up in a room with a locked door (John 20:19). So, though Jesus had a physical, material body that could eat and that Thomas was able to touch, He was also able to move through spiritual means. (See also Luke 24:31-43.)

Our physical bodies are bound by laws of nature. Believe me, I walk into walls and bang into shut doors all the time when I get disoriented. It doesn't go so well when you are trying to break the laws of nature while stuck in a natural body! But the resurrected Christ was not, and evidently we will not be either when we get our resurrected bodies. Or maybe the laws of nature as we know them are abolished.

How all this will unfold really is a mystery. But what is clear is that we will bear the image of "the man of Heaven"!

Read **1 Corinthians 15:48-49**.

Oh, sister, shake that dust off of you! Before you were found in Christ, you were of the dust. You were part of that first man, Adam. But no more. You are now in Christ. He is called the last Adam (v. 45) and is from Heaven, and He has prepared a place for you there to be with Him forever and ever.

I just imagine that if my body is buried when Christ returns, He will lift what is left of my remains from under the earth, and all the dust from that old grave will fall off like a cocoon from a butterfly. I'll bust out of that hard earth, lift my seeing eyes to Jesus as He transforms my weakness into power, my mortality into immortality, and my perishable into imperishable.

And I fully intend to pluck a blue flower from near my tombstone on my way out, grasping it tightly as I study each petal, until the moment I lay it at the feet of Jesus. And don't be surprised if I'm still wearing my GAP® denim jacket!

All right, tomorrow we'll finish up 1 Corinthians 15 and affirm that death is not the boss of us! Until then, my friend, peace be with you.

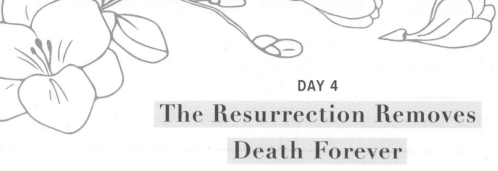

The Resurrection Removes
Death Forever

"He has met, fought, and beaten the King of Death. Everything is different because He has done so."[9]

C. S. LEWIS

I hope you're settled in with your Bible or your device where you read the Bible and a cup of something you enjoy. I've got steaming dark espresso in my yellow ceramic cup from Sorento, Italy. (I think the cup makes it taste even better.) I want to tell you a story my friend Lori recently told me about her friend Natalie. I can't wait to share it with you.

Natalie's husband died suddenly, leaving her and their three kids reeling with shock and heavy with grief. As they gathered at his grave with family and friends to say their goodbyes, the pastor was nowhere to be found. It was almost time to start. Melissa kept her eye on her watch and the parking lot, but no pastor. Finally with just one minute to spare, a black car sped in, the back door opened, and out stepped Pastor Jim.

He'd been Natalie's pastor for years, and he was also up in years. He had his own share of grief, having just buried his wife not many days before this funeral. He ambled up to the gathered mourners and greeted Natalie. He didn't hurry up and start, though. He looked around several times. His eyes gazed at the casket, then over the grieving, and finally into the grave. Then he startled everyone as he yelled into the abyss:

"Death, where is your sting? Grave, where is your victory?"

Silence followed. Only the rustling of the leaves could be heard. His voice became a megaphone again.

"Death, where is your sting? Grave, where is your victory?"

A holy hush fell on that place as those ten words blanketed each heart with comfort.

Later that evening, after the funeral was over and the loved ones were all back home, one of Natalie's daughters asked if she could go back to her daddy's grave. As they stood before that place where their beloved dad and husband lay, the daughter asked Natalie, "Can I do it?"

The newly widowed mom looked around, smiled through her tears at her girl, and said, "Sure, honey."

The daughter took a deep breath . . .

"Death, where is your sting? Grave, where is your victory?"

Over every silent grave, she yelled, "Death where is your sting? Grave, where is your victory?"

Through her pain and her grief, over her fears and loss, she yelled even louder . . .

"Death, where is your sting? Grave, where is your victory?"

Death had no response to that question because it is defeated. When the believer's body is swallowed by earth, death is swallowed by victory. Death does not have the final victory because death does not have the final voice. Jesus does.

Whew! I'm wiping away tears just typing that. So beautiful, right?

Lord, thank You for being the resurrection and the life. We do believe in You and are beyond thankful that though we may die, yet shall we live. Set our minds on things above today as we study Your Word. Amen (John 11:25; Col. 3:2).

Read **1 Corinthians 15:54-55**; **Hosea 13:14**; and **Isaiah 25:7-9** and take some notes comparing the three passages.

1 Cor DEATH HAS BEEN SWALLOWED UP
IN VICTORY
HOSEA REDEEMED FROM DEATH

ISAIAH HE WILL SWALLOW UP DEATH
FOREVER

Paul applied to Christ's resurrection what the Old Testament prophets had written hundreds of years earlier. Death has been swallowed up in victory. Death, where is your sting?

Before we study those words from the Word, we need to study our hearts for a minute. Let's be honest, death does sting. It hurts. Death, from our earthly perspective, looks like the winner. It doesn't appear to be defeated; rather, we are the ones who often feel powerless against it.

> What feelings most often accompany death, or the idea of death, for you? Why?
>
> GRIEF

For me, it's grief, confusion, sadness, and betrayal. Grief because there is just no reasoning away that deep sense of loss. Confusion because the feelings of grief and loss often are bewildering. I'm never quite sure how to navigate them. Sadness, well, I guess that is obvious. Death is such a tearing, a separation, that it leaves a hole in my soul, and my visceral response is just plain empty sorrow.

And lastly, betrayal. I don't feel betrayed by the person who died or even by God Himself. I choose the word *betrayal* because deep down, I just don't think it was supposed to turn out this way for the human race. We weren't created to die. Eden had no tombstones. We weren't intended to carry around grief.

But maybe what I call betrayal is rather a spiritual affirmation, a longing in disguise, the seeds of a blue flower. The resurrection proves we were not meant to die; we were created to be immortal, incorruptible, and clothed with the imperishable.

We may feel that sting of death. We may see with earthly eyes the finality of it. But then we stand by a tombstone on a mound of dirt and hear the echo of **1 Corinthians 15:57**.

> Read it out loud. It's okay if the dog or your coworker hears you!

God does lead us into victory. Not just victory over sin and death. He leads us into victory over and through the tough feelings that sting our souls.

Use your favorite Bible resource to find and then write some Scriptural victory declarations that correspond with the feelings you listed and on the previous page. For example, one of mine would be:

Grief: God is near to me when my heart is broken and my spirit is crushed (Ps. 34:18). He knows my sorrow and knows how I feel (Heb. 4:15).

_____ : _____

_____ : _____

_____ : _____

_____ : _____

_____ : _____

Assigning biblical truth to all the emotions that death brings can help us manage the emotional sting. That is part of the victory we have in Christ.

Jesus leads you into victory. He led you from death to life in salvation, and He will lead you back to hope if you feel crushed by all the feelings surrounding death. His Word can bring comfort and peace and assurance that death will not have the final word in your story or in your loved one's story. Thanks be to God!

Back to 1 Corinthians. Paul and the prophets were affirming that death has no sting. Yet the defeat of death doesn't just prove Christ's victory over the physical or material. His resurrection also proves He has victory over the spiritual.

Read 1 Corinthians 15:56. What do you think is the point Paul is making?

DEATH IS NO LONGER A SOURCE OF DREAD OR FEAR

Paul stated that the sting of death is sin. How do Genesis 2:17 and Romans 6:23 support that statement?

G YOU WILL DIE BECAUSE They ATE THE FORBIDDEN FRUIT
R WAGES OF SIN IS DEATH

Death is the result of sin. Sin is our ultimate cause of death. But you can't erase the result without eliminating the cause.

Jesus handled both on our behalf.

Jesus paid the price for our sin when He died on the cross. His sacrifice brought forgiveness.

Jesus broke the power of sin when He rose from the dead. Death no longer rules over Him or us.

So, death and sin no longer have power over you when you are in Christ. (Read Romans 6 for further study.) That's the reason for the proclamation worth shouting in verse 57:

> "But thanks be to God! He gives us the victory
> through our Lord Jesus Christ."

Let's pause and shout hallelujah! I'm doing it right along with you.

Finish up by reading the last verse of **1 Corinthians 15**.

In verse 58, it's like Paul, who has made a brilliant legal, social, and emotional case for Christ's and our resurrection for the last fifty-seven verses, pauses, takes a deep breath, and says "Therefore . . ."

As my pastor used to say, "What is the therefore there for?"

What is the final takeaway of this chapter?

Since you will rise then, stand firm now.

Since your future is secure, be steadfast in the present.

Since the grave won't hold you down someday, be immovable on this day.

Since the victory is already yours, give yourself one hundred percent to what God has called you to!

Oh, my friend, death does not have the final word because Jesus is the living Word (John 1). He is the resurrection and the life. If we believe in Him, though we die, yet shall we live (John 11:25).

Yet. Shall. We. Live! Take that, death!!

If you've lost somebody you love, maybe you still fight tears at his or her grave. Maybe you grieve so deeply still. Perhaps you need to go to that person's grave again and this time wipe your tears (or you can just let them flow! It's okay.), take a deep breath, and yell like that old preacher and that young daughter.

Death, where is your sting? Grave, where is your victory?

Then listen. You won't hear one thing because death has no voice except the one you give it. Don't let it lie to you any longer.

You do not need to fear death. You can grieve like a woman who has hope, because you do have hope (1 Thess. 4:13). You have hope that just like a sleeping child is awakened to a new morning and a new day, all of us in Christ, including you and your loved one, will be awakened someday to a forever, never-ending, eternal day.

Thank You, Lord, for victory through Jesus.

And all the sisters said? Amen and amen!

Well done sticking with the brilliant apostle Paul and all my attempts to understand him this week! Tomorrow, your *Takeaway Truths* and *Dash Living Day*.

Love you,

Jennifer

TAKEAWAY TRUTHS

Below are some important points we covered this week. There's also room for you to add other takeaways you want to remember.

- If Jesus was not resurrected, then we have no hope of being resurrected. But He has been resurrected!

- Jesus is the firstfruits of resurrection. Firstfruits is an agricultural term defined as the first part of the harvest that indicates and ensures future harvest is coming. Jesus's resurrection points to and guarantees that further resurrected bodies will follow.

- Though there were other people brought back to life in the Bible, none returned in a resurrected body. All came back in a normal human body that would eventually die again.

- Our resurrected bodies will be like Jesus's resurrected body—immortal, incorruptible, not bound by the laws of nature, yet still able to do physical things like eat and serve.

- Death and the grave are not the victors. Jesus is. Hallelujah!

RECORD YOUR DASH MEMORIES

On this *Dash Living Day*, start reflecting on and writing down some of your most special memories from your time here on earth so far. This will allow you to reflect on the goodness of God in your life and how He has worked or is working in your life.

This will also mean a lot to the people you love if you want to share it. Organize your memories in different ages or years. You may be twenty or eighty, yet every day of your beautiful life matters; enjoy recording some of your favorite Dash memories!

Below are some prompts you can use, or you can just write your thoughts in a journal. Take your time; don't feel like you have to do this in one sitting.

As a Child

- My favorite toy was:
- My favorite food was:
- My best memory about my childhood is:

As a Teenager

- I loved:
- I was embarrassed by:
- My favorite subject in school was:

In My Adult Years

- My favorite job has been:
- My toughest lesson to learn so far was:
- I laughed so hard when:
- The most fun thing I've ever done was:
- What I love most about God is:

"The memory of the righteous is a blessing . . ."

PROVERBS 10:7a (ESV)

GETTING READY TO RISE

BEFORE THE VIDEO

Welcome and Prayer

WATCH THE VIDEO

LISTEN, WILLIS: YOU MAY OR MAY NOT ___SLEEP___.

- When the Bible speaks of mystery, it's referring to something that had formerly been ___HIDDEN___ and has now been ___REVEALED___

WHAT IT LOOKS LIKE TO GRIEVE WITH (HOPE:)

- ___HURT___
- ___OFFER___ that hurt to God
- ___PRAY___
- ___EXPECT___

LISTEN, WILLIS: YOU WILL ___RISE___.

LISTEN, WILLIS: YOU WILL BE ___CHANGED___

- Death is not the final ___WORD___; Jesus is the ___living___ word. Therefore, death is ___defeated___

Go to **jenniferrothschild.com/heaven** to get an email summary of this video teaching in your inbox. Plus, while you're there, check out my *Heaven* playlist to help you look forward to your risen life forever with Jesus.

To access the video teaching sessions, use the instructions in the back of your Bible study book.

CONVERSATION GUIDE

PERSONAL BIBLE STUDY

- What was your favorite day of study? Why?

- Jennifer makes the statement, "It all rests on the resurrection." What does that mean and why is it so true?

- What does it mean that Christ is the firstfruits of the resurrection? Why is this such a hope-filled description for us?

- What is appealing to you about the resurrection body you will receive? Why?

- How has the cruel reality of death touched you and your family?

- Put into words the hope and joy you feel knowing Christ has defeated death.

- Which *Takeaway Truth* stands out to you and why?

- *Dash Living Day*: What were some of the favorite memories you recorded?

VIDEO TEACHING

- What's one thing that stood out to you from the video teaching? Why?

- Why is it important to acknowledge that death hurts in order to grieve with hope?

- Sometimes we choose to wallow in the pain of our grief rather than give it to God. Why do we do that and why is it not healthy?

- Share a personal example of how you've been able to grieve with hope.

- Do you look forward to Christ's return and our resurrection? If so, why? If not, why not?

SESSION FOUR

"For we live by faith, not by sight. We are confident, I say, and would prefer to be away from the body and at home with the Lord."

2 CORINTHIANS 5:7-8

GOT QUESTIONS?
THE BIBLE'S GOT ANSWERS

The subject of Heaven raises a lot of questions. So, this week we'll see how the Bible answers some of the most often asked questions about Heaven. We'll deal with the reality of Heaven and the nature of our relationships in Heaven (with God, others, and animals). You'll get comfort and clarity as we tenderly explore what Scripture says about what happens to those who die very young and those who take their own lives. A challenge to train your heart and thoughts to ask the best questions closes the week.

Ultimately, we'll acknowledge our greatest satisfaction comes not from getting answers about Heaven but from the revelation of and our relationship with the God of Heaven.

At Home with the Lord

"When the believer dies, the body goes into the grave; the soul and spirit go immediately to be with the Lord Jesus awaiting the body's resurrection, when they're joined together to be forever with the Lord in eternal bliss."[1]

CHARLES R. SWINDOLL

Pour your coffee or tea or grab your ice-cold fizzy glass of fun, and let's think about what happens when you die! I know, what a way to start this new week, right? But there's a one hundred percent chance it will happen (if Christ doesn't return before your last breath), so we might as well get real and deal with some questions about it.

Every time I visit my dad's grave, nestled under a sleepy oak tree draped with hanging moss flowers in a place called the "Garden of the Apostles," I wonder, *Dad, what are you doing right now? Have you reunited with Mama and Papa? Did you meet Hosea, Haggai, or Amos? What about the sweet baby I miscarried? Do you know her? Can you see me, Mom, and all our family?*

Have you wondered those kinds of things? Not only about the people who already died, but what it will be like for you when you die?

What kinds of questions do you have about Heaven?

We just spent a week learning that when Jesus returns, we will receive resurrection bodies and we'll move into our forever home on the new earth. (We'll talk about that even more next week.)

But every time I think of then, I think of now. Because honestly, most of the time when we think of death, our minds gravitate to the Heaven of now, not our forever Heaven—our forever home on the new earth.

The new earth glitters with splendor, awakens our imaginations, and pulses with excitement for sure. So, if we're not thoughtful or thorough, we may inadvertently diminish the true splendor and satisfaction of the present Heaven.

We may think the present Heaven is just a holding pen, like renting instead of owning, hanging out in the foyer before the worship service begins.

But that absolutely is not true.

The Heaven of now is what we've referred to as Paradise. It's the intermediate state.

And we've already affirmed through Scripture that when you close your eyes to this earth, you will be present with Jesus in that place. At that moment your faith becomes sight. Oh, it is no plain vanilla for sure!

But do you wonder what it will be like there and what form you will be in?

Lots of questions like these come up when we think of death and going to Heaven, right? There is so much we want to know, but there is so much we just can't know. The good news is that we will have a much clearer understanding when we see Jesus face to face and "shall know fully, even as [we are] fully known" (1 Cor. 13:12).

> Pause and consider what you know about Heaven so far. What are the most powerful truths or comforting realities about Heaven that have really stuck with you? (Remember, you can know something with certainty without understanding it completely.)

For me it's this: We will always be with the Lord. The what and when don't matter as much to me as the who and the where!

I know for certain the "who" of Heaven, and that I'll be with Him. That is enough for me.

Lord, whom have we in Heaven but You? There is nothing on earth we desire that is better than You. Our hearts and flesh may fail, but You are the strength of our lives. Strengthen us today in Your Word. Amen (Ps. 73:25-26).

Let's deal with two questions today:

QUESTION 1: Is the present Heaven a real place or just a spiritual concept?

Read **Acts 7:55-56**. Summarize Stephen's experience.

Wow. Stephen, full of the Holy Spirit, "looked intently into" (NASB) the present Heaven. He saw the glory of God and Jesus standing right there.

Stephen saw clearly into a spiritual dimension that fully existed. It was existing in a reality Stephen's eyes had never been opened to see before.

But other human eyes had seen this invisible realm.

Check out **2 Kings 6:17**.

When Elisha asked God to allow his servant to see the invisible, the servant saw the hills full of horses and chariots of fire.

Can you accept that there is a spiritual realm that presently exists beyond your ability to see and perhaps even comprehend? Jot down your thoughts and explain why or why not.

It's so hard to wrap our finite, earth-bound minds around something so abstract, that just beyond your ability to see is a bright, present reality of Heaven where God dwells.

I think blindness has helped me accept this truth. Here's why: I have blind eyes that cannot see what is right in front of me, yet my inability to see what is before me does not mean it does not exist. The point: there can be a very present reality beyond your ability to see, and proof of its existence is not affirmed by sight. Proof is affirmed by faith.

Pause for a moment, step outside, look up at the vast sky, and gaze into what you cannot see. Read **Amos 9:6** as you do and ask God to inform your imagination with His truth. Take as long as you need. I will wait!

Heaven exists. Jesus is there. My dad is there. Your loved one who died in Christ is there. It is the place where God dwells.

That leads to our second question.

QUESTION 2: What form will we be in if we die before Christ returns?

Since the present Heaven is a place, and God currently dwells there with the angels, what form are they in according to **John 4:24** and **Hebrews 1:14**?

God and angels are spirit beings. Even when Stephen looked into Heaven, he saw the "glory of God," rather than God Himself.

But what about Jesus? Twice Stephen said he saw Jesus standing in Heaven.

> Read **Acts 1:9-11**. Describe what form Jesus is in right now in the present Heaven based on these verses.

Jesus came to earth in a human body (John 1:14). His earthly body died and was raised as a resurrected body (1 Cor. 15:3-8). And in that body He ascended into Heaven (Acts 1:9-11).

So, it makes sense that Jesus reigns in His Father's house in a resurrected, glorified body.

But no one else has been resurrected yet. Paul made it clear in 1 Corinthians 15:52 that all believers will receive resurrected bodies "at the last trumpet," when Jesus returns. So, in what form does my dad and all the other righteous dead currently exist?

Hmmm, well, get ready for the best answer . . .

We don't know.

The Bible is not clear on this point. As we discussed back in Session One, Day Three, I do believe there IS biblical evidence for an intermediate state, where those who've died in Christ have conscious existence enjoying the presence of Christ, awaiting the resurrection. We based that understanding on the following passages:

- **Luke 16:19-31**, where Jesus told the parable of the rich man and Lazarus

- **Luke 23:43**, where Jesus promised to the thief on the cross that "today you will be with me in paradise"

- **2 Corinthians 5:6-8**, where Paul made it clear to be absent from this body is to be present with the Lord

- **Philippians 1:21-23**, where Paul proclaimed that for him to live is Christ, to die is gain and that he longed "to depart and be with Christ."

- **Revelation 6:9-11**, where John described the martyred saints crying out to the Lord

But let's pause here. While Luke 16 and Revelation 6 may indicate some form of embodiment for believers who die before Christ's return, consider the genre of literature for each of those passages.

Luke 16 is a parable. A parable is a short story designed to communicate a spiritual truth for principle. So, as noted earlier in the study, we need to be cautious about how literal we interpret what's written. And Revelation 6 is apocalyptic literature, which leans heavy on symbolism. So, though we shouldn't dismiss what we see in these passages, we also can't draw concrete conclusions either.

> Let's look at one other passage that relates to this question:
> **2 Corinthians 5:1-5**. Read and summarize these verses.

Paul stated in verse 1 that we know this earthly body (tent) is temporary and headed for destruction. It is not fit for Heaven. However, God is going to give us a new body that is fit for eternity ("an eternal house," NIV).

In the meantime, Paul echoed what we all know big time: we "groan" in this body (v. 2), longing for our eternal, incorruptible one (1 Cor. 15:53). We want to be "clothed," and "not be found naked" (v. 3).

So, honesty alert! I always thought this passage was referring to the type of "body" we would have in the intermediate state, but is it? Although there are some who think so, other scholars believe Paul is talking about the resurrected body we'll receive when Christ returns (1 Cor. 15:52; 1 Thess. 4:13-18). So, brace yourself; not even this passage definitively indicates what form we will be in in the present Heaven.

See why the best answer to this question is "we don't know"?

"We don't know" is not a bad answer. It's okay to not know details about something we are certain of. And what we are certain of is that we will have an animated existence, fully alive in the presence of Christ, but not yet all we will be in our resurrected bodies.

So, thank God for what you do know—you will be with the Lord. And trust Him with what you don't know and can't know because He's got you, sister!

All right, my cup is empty and my heart is full, so that's enough for now. Tomorrow we'll discuss what our relationships will be like in Heaven with people—and pets? Hmmm . . .

Until then, consider God's creative and redemptive work in you—worship Him, connect with Him, and thank Him that His Spirit has made you spiritually alive. So, live by His grace—Christ in you, THE hope of glory (Col. 1:27)!

Amen and amen!

> "May God Himself, the God of peace, sanctify you through and through.
> May your whole spirit, soul and body be kept blameless at the coming of
> our Lord Jesus Christ."
>
> **1 THESSALONIANS 5:23**

See you tomorrow!

DAY 2

At Home with Your People

"What we love about this life are the things that resonate with the life we were made for. The things we love are not merely the best this life has to offer—they are previews of the greater life to come."[2]

RANDY ALCORN

How do you capture memories? Are you like my hubby, a constant selfie taker? Believe me, if you've been with us, your cute face is probably smushed up against ours in a selfie on his camera roll! Or maybe you film lots of videos? Or maybe you print your pics and place them artfully in albums? (Way to go, you!)

I take lots of audio pictures—snippets of life's sounds I capture on my phone. They are each less than a minute long, and I keep them and listen to them to remember things I love about life. It's the audio equivalent of pics on your phone that you scroll through.

I decided to share some of my favorite audio pictures on my *4:13* podcast. One of the most popular audio picture episodes is called, "The Good Life: The Dog, People, and Moments I Love." It's real life behind-the-scenes audio of, well, the dog, the people, and random moments I love! I guess that was obvious?

All those good things we capture on audio, video, or images represent what brings us joy. But those good things are just shadows, glimpses, seeds of the blue flower. They represent a longing that will one day be complete and a joy that will be fully realized. They are not the point; they are pointers. They point to the reality of Heaven and all we'll experience when our faith becomes sight.

So, if people and pets and family and spouses are all part of our good life here, will they be part of our best life there in the present and forever Heaven? And if so, how? Let's take a look by answering three questions. But first, let's pray.

Lord, we ask You for wisdom and we trust You will grant us
what we need to rightly divide Your Word. Amen (James 1:5-6;
2 Tim. 2:15).

QUESTION 1: Will I be married in Heaven?

Depending on how you feel about marriage, if you're married, or how you feel about your spouse, you may be hoping for a very distinct answer. If your marriage is difficult, you may be hoping for a negative answer. And for you, that would be a relief.

But if you're in a fulfilling marriage, you may not think Heaven can be Heaven without being married. Or if you are single or single again, and you long for a satisfying marriage, you may be holding out hope that even if you don't experience a good marriage here on earth, maybe you will on the new earth. Wow. So many emotions associated with this question.

Let's press pause on the emotion of this and consider what the Bible says.

> First, what are the purposes of marriage according to **Genesis 2:18** and **9:7**?
>
> ☐ To delegate toilet repairs or dinner prep
> ☐ To propagate the human race
> ☐ Companionship

Marriage includes lots of good stuff (including toilet repairs), but two of the main purposes are not being alone and populating the earth.

> Now read **Mark 12:25** and summarize what Jesus said about marriage in our forever Heaven.

Jesus made it clear that in our risen life we won't marry or be given in marriage. Rather, we will be like the angels, who neither marry nor procreate. (Notice Jesus didn't say we would BECOME angels, but we will be LIKE angels in our status as unmarried.)

But if marriage is part of our good life here, why won't we experience it in our best life ever in Heaven?

> What needs are met through marriage that will not exist in Heaven, and why? (See **Isa. 54:5** and **Hos. 2:19-20**.)

Marriage will not exist in the same way because its intended purpose will be perfected when we are united fully with Christ in Heaven. In other words, you will be united with Christ in Heaven and have no need for the benefits earthly marriage provides. The picture of marriage now (the union of Christ and His bride, the church, Eph. 5:22-23) will no longer need to serve as a pointer because we will be living the point! We will be made one with Christ forever. However, that doesn't mean that the close, loving relationship you had or have with your spouse will not have some echo in Heaven.

So, let your beautiful marriage be a blue flower that causes you to look forward to the perfect union that is yours someday with Christ. If you ache for marriage or a fulfilling, safe marriage, let that longing awaken a certain anticipation that you will experience the perfect union you were made for when your faith becomes sight. In other words, if you bank your whole life on the resurrection, you will not be disappointed, whether you marry in this life or not.[3]

All the longings we feel for deep, satisfying relationships point to the real point: God put them there so you would desire Him above all. Then when He, and He alone, fulfills those longings, you will fully adore Him.

> Study your heart and then journal your thoughts or jot down a prayer about this before you move on.

All this leads to another question.

QUESTION 2: Will we recognize each other in the present and forever Heaven?

Before you answer, let me ask you some questions.

- Will you be less you in Heaven than you are now?

- Will you be fully you in Heaven?

- Will you be the best version of you in Heaven?

What are your thoughts?

You will be more you than you've ever been because there will be no sin to constrain, drain, and mess with your brain! You'll be like that seed that is buried and then blossoms into its full potential and created intent (1 Cor. 15:36-38).

That being true, I ask: Do you recognize your people now? Of course you do!

Now, read **1 Corinthians 13:12** and describe how this verse suggests we will experience Christ and others when this earthly veil is lifted.

Just so we're clear, the following is speculation on my part: it makes no sense to me that memories will be erased in Heaven. Instead, because we will know as we are known, perhaps our memories will be expanded. All those times you can't recall a name, or wonder why you walked into a room, or wish you could remember what that person told you in your last conversation, none of that will be a thing.

Read **Matthew 17:1-4**. What about this scene makes no earthly sense to you?

Here are some options:

- Peter (and we assume James and John) recognized men they'd never met or seen.

- Elijah and Moses appeared in some kind of embodiment.

Peter and his cohorts recognized those prophets, just as they recognized Jesus in His transfigured state. They also recognized Jesus after He was resurrected.

I've gotta say, none of that makes earthly sense to me! Recognizing people you've never seen before? But that doesn't mean it isn't absolutely true. Based on all Scripture shows us, it seems we will know and recognize each other in Heaven.

At least the humans. But what about Mittens and Fido?

QUESTION 3: Will there be animals in Heaven?

It was a Wednesday morning, while writing on Heaven, that I cradled my little Shih Tzu Lucy as the vet administered a sedative to prepare her for her passing. Lucy was a dear old girl of 16 who sat on my desk as a fluffy black and white puppy and watched me write *Me, Myself & Lies* many years ago. Yet, Sweet Girl was not well and long for this earth, so we made the hardest best decision to make her comfortable and end her suffering.

As she lay on my lap, I thought she didn't have the energy to even lift her cute head until the vet placed a bowl of squeeze cheese on the pillow by her mouth to distract Lucy from the injection. That diva dog sucked up that cheese with the vigor of a puppy! But it was her last hurrah. As I felt her heart slow and heard her breathing change, fighting back my own tears, I wondered, will Lucy be in Heaven when I get there?

Let's be super honest. Most of us wonder if our pets will be with us for eternity, don't we? We love them and want them to be there.

What do you think?

What do you base your thoughts on? Scripture? Your desires? Culture? Emotion? Logic?

The Bible doesn't say emphatically, so let's discern the biblical principle.

According to **Genesis 1:24-25**, how do you think God feels about animals?

Animals were part of God's original creation, and He called them "good."

Then when the earth was to be flooded, note what He commanded in **Genesis 6:17-20**.

When God was renewing His creation after the flood, He intended for animals to be with Noah and his family.

So, if animals were important to God for this earth, it's probable they will also be important for the new earth, our forever Heaven.

Maybe our affection for animals here is not the point, but it points to an even more beautiful satisfaction.

Lucy brought me joy and companionship. She was a perfect little earthly need-meeter in those areas. Yet, in Heaven, both the present and forever Heaven, I will no longer have those needs because they will be met by Christ.

Does that mean animals are only for utility? Can they also be for our delight and God's glory, especially in our forever Heaven of the new earth?

Look at the poetic picture Isaiah draws in **Isaiah 11:6–9.** Jot down your observations about the kinds of animals and how they relate to each other. Describe what this scene communicates about what the earth will be like when it is full of the knowledge of the Lord (v. 9).

Listen to the 4:13 Podcast Good Life episode to hear my audio pictures of the dog, people, and moments I love at **413podcast.com/GoodLife4.**

The presence of animals, along with vulnerable little children in their midst, illustrates a peace, rightness, and restoration of God's original creative intent that we all long for.

Oh my friend, I don't know for certain about animals in Heaven. As I mentioned earlier, the Bible is not emphatic on that point. But perhaps it's not emphatic because there is an underlying assumption: If animals were part of the original creation of earth, why wouldn't they be part of the eventual restoration of earth?

And Lucy? Well, I certainly don't know for sure, but I have a feeling if there is squeeze cheese, she will be there!

If any of these questions or answers leave you longing or wishing or wondering, let those feelings be paths to greater wisdom, not pitfalls or potholes you stumble over and get stuck in. Don't shame yourself at this point in your journey if your longing to hang out with your hubby or children or beloved pet in Heaven is greater than your desire to be with Jesus. Ask God to keep developing in you the greatest longing that will be utterly satisfied: to be united with Christ, the true Treasure of Heaven—to know as you are known, your faith finally sight.

Lord, in Your presence there is fullness of joy. At Your right hand are pleasures forever and ever and ever. Help us to let all the pointers move our heart toward the real point—Jesus, our risen Lamb. To Him be praise. Amen (Ps. 16:11).

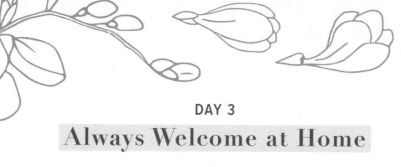

Always Welcome at Home

"We are not far from home. Heaven . . . is just one sigh and we get there. Our departed friends are only in the upper room, as it were, of the same house; they have not gone far off; they are upstairs and we are down below."[4]

CHARLES SPURGEON

I'm sitting at my kitchen table, imagining you right across from me. My steaming cup of coffee makes our setting so fragrant and warm. (I hope you like coffee or at least the aroma!)

I like to think of you right there so I can reach over and place my hand on yours. I want you to be prepared emotionally. In fact, you may want to pass on this day of study, at least for the moment. Or maybe do it at another time with a Bible study buddy. The subject is hard. We're going to talk about Heaven as it relates to infant death and suicide. My friend, I have had up-close experience with both, so I promise I'll gently walk us through this day.

So, if you're up for this, take a deep breath, take a sip of your coffee, and ask God to guide us as our gentle Shepherd.

Lord, You are our Shepherd. We will not fear, even when we walk through dark valleys, because we know You are with us. Comfort us today. Amen (Ps. 23).

QUESTION 1: Do babies and children too young to choose Christ go to Heaven when they die?

I'll never forget explaining my miscarriage to our nine-year-old son, Clayton. How do you tell a little boy, who has longed for and prayed for a brother, that you aren't going to have the baby after all? How do you explain to a child that the baby we thought was to be born and add such joy to our family is not alive?

And how do we explain this to our own hearts, the ones who carry the babies, carry the hope, and then have to carry the grief and loss? Plus, the ones who carry the weight of disappointment and the burden of sharing the sad news with others? Some things are just inexplicable to the heart even when the head understands.

I will never forget the nerves I felt before telling Clayton about the miscarriage just hours after returning from the hospital. I sat next to him on our mauve-flowered couch and the words just tumbled out—*our baby won't be born on earth because our baby was born in Heaven.* That made sense to Clayton, and in a weird way, it made sense to my heart. But now I wonder if it makes sense biblically.

I also think of my friend whose nephew lived only three months outside the womb because of failing, fragile lungs. Is he in Heaven?

> Let's see what the Bible says about this. What principle about children did Jesus portray in **Matthew 19:14**?

> King David lost a baby and felt the weight of grief. What do David's words in **2 Samuel 12:23** suggest about infant death?

> Based on Jesus's and David's words, how would you comfort someone grieving the loss of a baby or child?

My words to Clayton may be a childlike summary, but I do think, based on Scripture, they represent the heart of God. Jesus called little children to Himself. He loved them and blessed them. When David's baby died, David knew that he would one day join that baby in his Father's house. Even though a preborn baby or a small child has a sin nature, as every human does, they haven't developed the intellectual capacity to choose to agree with that nature and reject God. Therefore, the finished work of Christ on the cross comforts us in knowing where those little ones are if they die. They are safe in His arms. When we can't understand what God allows, we can still trust Who He is. We rest in His kind, compassionate character. I certainly don't understand God's ways, but with all my heart, I trust His heart. That is my prayer for you also.

If the sorrow and loss of miscarriage has shaken you or someone you love, may God be your comfort and give you hope. Don't hesitate to reach out for wise counsel to help you process your loss because your loss is real. Even though no one held that sweet baby in their arms, you held him or her in your heart and that matters. May those who have not been touched by miscarriage show the compassion and empathy of Jesus to those who have.

One other thing: we don't know if those who die in the womb or as young children remain as babies or young children in the intermediate state. We don't know if they are full-grown adults by the time we get to the new earth or if they will grow up there. Sister, We. Do. Not. Know. The Bible does not say. So let that question go. Instead, focus on the good character and heart of God who is not willing that any should perish. Trust Jesus as the Good Shepherd who makes sure all His little lambs are safe with Him.

That's comforting truth for sure.

But what happens to those who take their own lives?

Question 2: Does the Christian who dies by suicide still go to Heaven?

Hearing the raw and unrestrained wails of young men in their twenties gathered around their friend's casket broke my heart into a million pieces. Especially since one of those young men was my son, Clayton. He was mourning the loss of his lifelong friend Wesley. When I heard the grieving cries of my friend, Wesley's mother, I lost it completely. Such deep anguish. We all loved Wesley and were so heartbroken that this precious young man died by suicide. When I remember that dark day, my mind races through so many others I have lost to suicide—friends from church, friends from college—all Christians.

After a college friend died by suicide, I'll never forget a mutual friend commenting to me that those who die by suicide can't go to Heaven. She based this belief on 1 John 1:9—that people who take their own lives commit a sin with no time to confess or repent. I was a mix of sorrow and rage and frustration over such a misunderstanding and misapplication of that verse.

Let's see what the Bible says about this.

First, let's start with a hard question. Is suicide a sin?

> Read **1 Corinthians 6:19-20** and **Exodus 20:13**.
>
> According to the principles in those verses, is suicide a sin? Yes or no? Explain.

When we belong to Christ, it's the total package, including our bodies! We are not our own. So, to take our own lives is to sin against the body that belongs to Christ.

Yet are there other sins we commit against our bodies?

> Read **1 Corinthians 6:18**. What sin against the body is addressed in this verse?

Sex outside biblical boundaries is sin against the body too.

> What did Paul say in **1 Thessalonians 4:3-4** about how we treat our bodies?

Staying sexually pure isn't just a good idea; it is God's will for each of us. Through God's grace, we can learn to control our bodies in ways that are holy and honorable.

Oh, my friend, we all sin, and sometimes that sin is against our bodies. And all sin is against God (Ps. 51:4; Rom. 3:23). Suicide is a sin. Sex outside biblical boundaries is a sin. And so is gossip, gluttony, lying, rage, greed, and I could go on and on and on. (But I'd really rather not. Okay with you?)

Here is the really big question: Are all those sins forgivable?

But what if you don't confess each and every one every time you commit one? Are you still forgiven?

> Read **Psalm 103:10-12** and **Ephesians 1:7-8**. Summarize God's perspective of and action toward our sin and what our forgiveness is based on.

Our forgiveness is according to the riches of God's grace for those who "fear" Him—in other words, for those who are in Christ.

First Corinthians 15:3 reminds us that Christ died for our sins—all the ugly lot of them—past, present, and future. (See also Gal. 1:3-4 and 1 Pet. 2:24.)

Once we are in Christ, we are positionally, judicially forgiven. First John 1:9 speaks of relational confession and restoration within the context of judicial and positional forgiveness.

When we receive Christ, all our sins, past, present, future, are washed away. We are now in a relationship with God that can never be broken. However, we still struggle with sin. And though this sin doesn't change our eternal relationship with God, it does mess with our fellowship with Him. Think of it this way: My son will always be my son. Nothing he does will change that relationship. But if he lies to me, our fellowship is broken. Our emotional connection would certainly change, but the relationship status would not and could never change. He is my son. Period. He would remain positionally, legally, unconditionally my son who I love. Once we are in Christ, we are safe in the love of God—positionally accepted and forgiven whether we have time to confess immediate sin or not.

If our eternal salvation were based on our ability to confess every sin every time just in time, then, sister, we are not saved by grace. That is salvation based on works. My work, not the work of Christ.

Suicide is one sin of many sins. Jesus died for all sin. And those who die knowing Christ, no matter how they die, can trust the truth of Jude 24-25.

> Write out **Jude 24-25** in first person as a praise to God and a comfort for you. Or if you love someone who knew Christ and died by suicide, use their name in those verses.

God is able to present us faultless before His throne because of Christ's righteousness, regardless of our final earthly action. To Him be praise.

My friend, those of us who haven't fought the battle with suicidal despair need to humbly listen to those who have. Those who die by suicide, or love someone who did, are often fighting battles beyond what we can imagine. So, there is no shame piled on anyone who struggles or to anyone who has lost someone they love to suicide. There is only grace, love, and support.

For hope-filled encouragement about loss from suicide, listen to **413Podcast.com/119** where we answer the question, "Can I find life again after someone I love lost his life to suicide?"

If you or someone you love is struggling with this, please tell somebody. Reach out to your pastor, a Christian counselor, or if you live in the United States, call 988.

I know what we've talked about today may have been hard and even heartbreaking for you. It was really about one thing: loss. The loss of lives is tragic and unfathomable. It feels wrong to us because Eden had no tombstones. Before the fall, there was no sin. No suffering. No sorrow. Babies didn't die. Young men didn't end their own lives. Yet between Eden and our eternal home, we live with loss. But not without hope. So, bring it all to Jesus. Bring your sorrow, your loss, your questions, your regrets. Bring it all to Him.

> "Here bring your wounded hearts, here tell your anguish;
> earth has no sorrow that Heaven cannot heal."[5]
>
> **COME, YE DISCONSOLATE**, THOMAS MOORE

My friend, the hope of Heaven can help heal the wounds of earth. Let that loved one live in your past memory and in your future anticipation, knowing you will be together with them and with the Lord someday.

"For I am convinced that neither death nor life, neither angels nor demons, neither the present nor the future, nor any powers, neither height nor depth, nor anything else in all creation, will be able to separate us from the love of God that is in Christ Jesus our Lord."

ROMANS 8:38-39

DAY 4
Let the Questions Guide You Home

"If we knew as much about Heaven as God does, we would clap our hands every time a Christian dies."[6]

GEORGE MACDONALD

We've asked lots of specific questions about Heaven this week. But today I want to start with kind of a random question. Before I do, get your coffee or tea, your Bible, put on your comfy pants, and let's start with prayer.

Lord, search us and know us and open our hearts so we can search and know ourselves as we study Your Word and our hearts today. Amen (Ps. 139:23-24).

Here's the question:

Have you ever heard of biblical typology? (I know, random, but you'll see how this fits.) If not, look it up in your favorite Bible resource, or just search online about it. What is it?

First, typology in general is a kind of symbolism. Remember, a symbol is a representation of the real thing, not the real thing itself. In the Bible, typology refers to a person, thing, or event in the Old Testament that foreshadows a person, thing, or event in the New Testament.

Now, continuing your research in your Bible reference or internet search, find the meaning of "Type of Christ in the Old Testament."

Explain and jot down some examples.

A type of Christ is not a variation of, an embodiment of, or a kind of Christ. The term refers to people, things, or events who prefigure, foreshadow, or point to who Christ is.

Some examples include Adam, Joshua, Job, Jacob's ladder, the bronze serpent, and more.

Choose a couple of these examples and explain how they are types of Christ.

Adam was the first man. Joshua saved his people. Job suffered righteously. The bronze serpent foreshadowed Jesus being raised to save us. Jesus was the ultimate "Jacob's Ladder," the connection between Heaven and earth.

How about Solomon? Stick with me. This will make sense in a minute.

Solomon was also a type of Christ. Can you think of some reasons why?

Solomon was a king, the son of David. He was the first fulfillment of the Davidic covenant. Jesus is the ultimate fulfillment of that covenant as the King of kings, the Son of David who sits on the throne forever. Solomon was wise. Jesus is the wisdom of God. Solomon built the temple; Jesus is the true and greater temple.

Wow. Right?

Now, here is where the seemingly random takes shape.

Find Matthew 12:42. Summarize what Jesus is talking about and who He is connecting Himself with.

Jesus acknowledged the connection with Solomon when he referred to the Queen of Sheba. She came from the ends of the earth to get wisdom. Now, Gentiles, all people from everywhere, come to seek the wisdom of the greatest Solomon—Jesus.

Alright, now that you're practically a typology expert, you may wonder why we're talking about this in a study of Heaven. So glad you asked! We have asked some hard questions this week, seeking wisdom from God's Word much like the Queen of Sheba sought wisdom from Solomon. Yet I want us to see what she found by asking.

Let's read her story in **1 Kings 10:1–9.**

What had she heard about Solomon and why did she travel to find him?

She heard about Solomon's fame and his relationship with God, so she came to ask him hard questions. She got far more than just answers though.

Summarize what the queen learned about God after asking her questions (10:9).

Sheba asked hard questions but got more than mere answers. She received a clear view of God as worthy of praise—sovereign in all He does, generous and loving, purposeful, concerned with justice and righteousness. Her curiosity and commitment to ask questions revealed a treasure far better than answers. It revealed God.

So, think of the kinds of questions we ask about Heaven. They reflect our curiosity. And hopefully they lead us to a revelation of God. But did you ever consider that our questions also can reveal our hearts?

Here's what I mean: This morning an article popped into my inbox. The subject line read: "Will Heaven Be Boring?"

Interesting question, right? But I felt an odd, uncomfortable reaction to it that I didn't expect, and wasn't sure why. I went online and searched for top questions about Heaven, and there it was—in the top five of most lists! It's a common curiosity, So, why was I so weirded out by it?

Now, let's pause here before I answer. If you have asked that question, I am not judging you, I promise. Clearly, you are in the top five of questioners about Heaven!

But that question made me uncomfortable because it exposed my heart. It spotlighted my selfish focus. When I asked that question in the past, it wasn't because I cared about the answer; it was because I cared about me. I wanted Heaven to be what I wanted it to be.

If I am the first and most constant thing on my mind, my questions about Heaven will be self-centered. *Will I like it? Will it meet my needs?* Let's be real with each other; we often make Heaven all about us—our ideal scenario according to our ideal definition, with a very big capital "I."

It's not that a question that primarily relates to me is inherently bad. No way. It's just that the question is incomplete in and of itself. Our questions are most effective if we are humble enough and vulnerable enough to let the questions reveal our hearts and lead us to greater understanding of ourselves and God as we listen to Him speak.

So, as we wind up this week, let's study our hearts by considering the questions we ask, why we ask them, and what they reveal about what we treasure. Because, sister to sister, it would be such a loss if we only get some good info about the afterlife and miss the deeper purpose of asking questions. We would maybe be a little smarter about Heaven but no closer to the God of Heaven. We want to be like the Queen of Sheba—seek and ask but get something far better than mere answers—a clear revelation of God.

Take a moment to pray and journal your thoughts about the following:

What are my biggest questions about Heaven?

What do each of those questions reveal about my heart or what I treasure?

Are there some better questions I can begin to ask about Heaven? If so, what are they?

How can I better live with eternity in mind, and why is it important?

My friend, the deeper purpose for asking questions about Heaven is strengthening connection with God, not just getting answers from Him.

Let's be like the Queen of Sheba. Ask good questions. Seek answers but open our hearts and anticipate getting something far better than an answer—a more clear revelation of God. May our hearts be revealed through the questions and refined by God's Spirit. May our hearts gravitate toward the true and only source of eternal deep satisfaction, rather than settle for satisfying answers. May we be more eternity-minded, living for kingdom purposes, and seeking the treasure of Heaven, Jesus.

Well, this week is a wrap! Tomorrow we will take a breath and do some *Dash Living*!

Great job this week. Next week we are moving into the new earth!

But first, check out your *Takeaway Truths* and enjoy watching the video teaching with your Bible study buddies!

TAKEAWAY TRUTHS

Below are some important points we covered this week. There's also room for you to add other takeaways you want to remember.

- Believers who die before the return of Christ exist in a recognizable form before receiving resurrected bodies when Christ returns.

- Scripture indicates we will know and recognize people in Heaven and will have relationships, but not marriage relationships. The needs that marriage currently meets will be totally fulfilled in Christ.

- It is unclear whether our pets will be present in Heaven, but there is scriptural evidence that indicates animals will be present on the new earth.

- Based on what we know from Scripture concerning the character and heart of God, babies and children too young to choose Christ go to Heaven when they die.

- Suicide is not an unforgivable sin. Believers who take their own lives are not judged by their last earthly act. If they have trusted Christ, they go to be with Him when they die.

- It's good to ask questions about Heaven. But as we ask, let's evaluate our motives, asking God-centered questions with sincere hearts.

MY BLESSINGS

Too often we leave things unsaid before we, or someone close to us, passes away. Here's a chance to record blessings you can both pass along now and leave behind. Perhaps you want to give a blessing to your daughter or encourage your pastor or work colleague. This exercise can serve as a reminder and depository of how others have impacted you. It will capture your heart, bless the ones who read it, and allow the power of your words to be felt deeply as current and future encouragement.

Fill in the name of someone you want to bless in each blank below and complete each sentence. You can do it exactly as it's written or use it as an adaptable guide.

If you make multiple copies of this page, you can fill out each blank for just one loved one! Insert all your copies here so your loved ones can read all the blessings you leave behind. But also, let the list motivate you to find ways to encourage each person now.

MY BLESSINGS

I appreciate _____ because _____

I admire _____ because _____

I respect _____ because _____

I trust _____ because _____

I enjoy _____ because _____

I observe _____

I am confident _____

I believe _____

I applaud _____

I treasure _____

"I thank my God every time I remember you."

PHILIPPIANS 1:3

MAKING JESUS THE TREASURE OF HEAVEN

BEFORE THE VIDEO

Welcome and Prayer

WATCH THE VIDEO

The true treasure of Heaven is _____.

TWO WAYS WE MAKE JESUS THE TREASURE OF HEAVEN:

1. **Seek the _____.**

   • We need to let the _____ lead us to the point.

2. **_____ in Him.**

   • If we _____ in Him now, then it will be a _____ with Him then.

   • Remaining in Jesus is not just about our _____ in Him, but our _____ to Him.

If Jesus becomes our treasure of _____, He will be our treasure on _____.

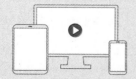

To access the video teaching sessions, use the instructions in the back of your Bible study book.

CONVERSATION GUIDE

PERSONAL BIBLE STUDY

- What was your favorite day of study? Why?

- Are you able to accept there's a spiritual realm that exists beyond what you can see and perhaps comprehend? If yes, what enables you to do so? If not, what hinders you?

- When it comes to questions you have about Heaven, what are you basing your current answers on?

- How would you counsel and comfort someone who's wrestling with the sensitive questions about the eternal destination of young children and/or Christians who die by suicide?

- Consider the questions you ask about Heaven. Why do you think you're asking them? Does that matter? Explain.

- Which *Takeaway Truth* stands out to you and why?

- *Dash Living Day*: Share some of the blessings you listed and why.

VIDEO TEACHING

- What's one thing that stood out to you from the video teaching? Why?

- What is meant by the statement that the true treasure of Heaven is Jesus?

- How do the beautiful things in our lives sometimes get in the way of seeing the main point, which is Jesus? How are these things pointers to what's most important?

- What does it mean to remain in Jesus? How is remaining in Him not just about position but also proximity?

- What is the evidence in our lives that Jesus is our true treasure?

SESSION FIVE

"Then I saw 'a new heaven and a new earth,' for the first heaven
and the first earth had passed away, and there was no longer
any sea. I saw the Holy City, the new Jerusalem, coming down
out of heaven from God, prepared as a bride beautifully dressed
for her husband. And I heard a loud voice from the throne saying,
'Look! God's dwelling place is now among the people, and he will
dwell with them. They will be his people, and God himself will be
with them and be their God. 'He will wipe every tear from their
eyes. There will be no more death' or mourning or crying or pain,
for the old order of things has passed away.' He who was seated
on the throne said, 'I am making everything new!' Then he said,
'Write this down, for these words are trustworthy and true.'"

REVELATION 21:1-5

OUR FOREVER HOME

We'll spend most of this week in Revelation, John the apostle's record of the vision he received concerning "what must soon take place" (Rev. 1:1). We will especially focus on chapters 21 and 22 to discover what our forever home will be like. We'll take a brief look at the final judgment, then deal mainly with the nature of our eternal experience on the new earth. We'll grow in anticipation of being united with all the redeemed from every tribe, tongue, and nation and find hope in the reality of what we will "no longer" deal with and what will be "no more."

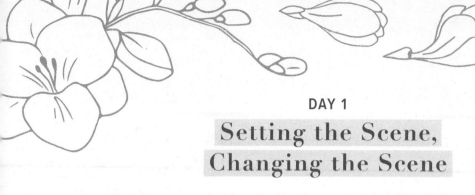

Setting the Scene, Changing the Scene

"Now at last they were beginning Chapter One of the Great Story which no one on earth has read: which goes on forever: in which every chapter is better than the one before."[1]

C. S. LEWIS

Hurry to your seat. It's almost time. We're in the theatre. The lights are low. The crowd hums with barely containable anticipation.

You're just in time, so don't stress. Look around. Do you see all the people? You're not the only one waiting for the curtain to open. Everyone in this place is hyped for this moment.

Then it starts. You hear it before you see it.

A trumpet sounds. The crowd gasps.

Then a shout. The audience applauds. You are filled with joy, and you can't take your eyes off the scene that is about to unfold before you. This is the moment you've waited for.

The curtain opens . . .

> Now freeze frame that image in your imagination for just a sec. If you are sitting in one of those seats waiting for your most favorite artist, author, or entertainer to appear, just for fun I want to know: who is behind that curtain?

For me, it would be Lionel Ritchie. Oh, and C. S. Lewis! That would be quite a combo, right?

There's no satisfaction quite like the satisfaction you feel when a long-awaited anticipation is realized.

I felt it the first time I got to see Lionel in concert. Girl, I was so excited I was at risk of a restraining order. And oh, the first time I went to Oxford, England to C. S. Lewis's home, The Kilns, I fought back tears. I was so full of joy from a longing fulfilled.

We probably all understand that feeling of anticipation. And you are supposed to feel it— to feel the ache for the longing to be fulfilled.

There is a longing God has put in each of His children and even in nature itself (Rom. 8:19-23) to see the One our souls love on "that day."

Let's ask God to give us clarity about that day, because "that day" will usher in forever days with Him.

> *Lord, may we be humble and tremble at Your Word today as we study. Amen (Isa. 66:2).*

Parousia. (Puh-ROO-see-uh)

Whaaat? If that's Greek to you, there's a reason. It's Greek.

> Grab your favorite Bible resource again or start that internet search to find out what it means. Better yet, read the following verses and see if you can determine what *parousia* means based on common words.
>
> **Hebrews 9:28**
>
> **2 Timothy 4:8**

Parousia comes from two Greek words which mean to come and be present. It denotes an appearing, an arrival along with an ensuing presence.

In the context of this study, when we talk *parousia*, we're talking about the day the curtains of history are flung open to reveal Jesus.

Trying to discern and understand what's going to happen on that day and leading up to that day are what we call eschatology or a study of the last days.

Perhaps you're interested in that. Me too.

However, as stated before, this Bible study is not a study about end times. So, we're not going to do a deep dive into what happens or the timing of what happens before we get to our eternal home on the new earth, our forever Heaven. Our focus is on what happens when we get there.

But I get it; we're curious. So let me summarize the four basic views of what leads up to our moving into the new earth. As a reminder, what end times view you hold is not a primary issue. We can hold different views and still walk together in faith and fellowship.

FOUR VIEWS OF END TIMES

The four most common views center around how each understands the millennium, the one thousand year reign of Christ spoken of in Revelation 20:1-10. The following information is not an exhaustive explanation but a brief snapshot of each view.

1. **Postmillennial View:** Postmillenialists don't necessarily view the one thousand year period as literal, rather as just a long period of time. In fact, most who hold this view believe it to be the current age we're living in—from the ascension of Christ until His return. Others believe the reign is still to come, but still along the same timeline of our current history. They take an optimistic view believing that the world will get better and better as more and more people come to Christ. Once the world is Christianized, Jesus will return, the resurrection of the dead and final judgment will take place, followed by our eternal state.

2. **Amillennial Perspective:** Those who hold this view see the one thousand year reign as symbolic, that it began at Christ's resurrection when He became victorious over death and the curse and extends until He returns. Unlike postmillennialists, they don't see the world getting better and the culture changing to be more Christian. Instead, as the end gets closer, they see evil becoming more prevalent, including a time of tribulation. Then at some point, Christ returns, the dead are resurrected, the final judgment takes place, followed by our eternal state on the new earth.

3. **Dispensation Premillennial View:** Those holding this view believe there will be a literal one thousand year reign of Christ. It will be preceded by the rapture of the church. In the rapture, (which literally means "to snatch"), Christ doesn't come all the way to earth but meets the church (believers who are alive and the dead in Christ who will be resurrected) in the air. Following that event comes a great tribulation period.

After the tribulation, Jesus will return to earth and reign for one thousand years. Then comes the final judgment and the inauguration of the new heavens and new earth.

4. **Historic Premillennial View:** This view shares most of the same points as dispensational premillennialism, except the resurrection of the saints and rapture of the church do not take place before the tribulation. Instead they happen simultaneously with the return of Christ after the tribulation and before the literal one thousand year reign. As with dispensationalism, the one thousand year reign is followed by the final judgment, then the new heavens and new earth.

   After reading the summary of each end times view, what do the views have in common?

Each of the viewpoints gets there differently, but each eventually ends up at the same place: the final judgment and then the eternal state (new heavens, new earth). This is what I playfully called our strawberry fields forever!

So, before we step into the new earth, we have to stop at the final judgment. Buckle up, butter cup, here we go.

Final Judgment

Regardless of which last days' view we take, Scripture is clear there will be a final judgment (Dan. 12:2; John 5:24-30; Heb. 9:27).

   Read **Revelation 20:11-15** and then in the squares below draw images depicting this final judgment scene. Or if you're not feeling artsy, summarize the events described in this passage.

Images of a great white throne, lots of people, the book of life, the sea, death and Hell, and a lake of fire all come into focus as we see this scene unfold. You might be wondering how this judgment relates to the *bema* judgment for believers we talked about on Day Four of Session Two (p. 69). There is a debate among scholars on the number of judgments and who will be at the white throne judgment. Some see the *bema* judgment and the white throne judgment as separate events, with only believers in Christ at the *bema* judgment and only those who are not in Christ at this final judgment. While others see all people, believers and unbelievers ("the great and small," v. 12), gathered before the great white throne and both judgments taking place at the same time. One thing is clear about this passage though—the separation that takes place. Those whose names are written in the book of life—those who've trusted in Christ for salvation—move on to the new heavens and the new earth. But those whose names are not listed there are headed for eternal destruction. They are thrown into the lake of fire, along with the devil (20:10) and death and Hades (20:14). Whew! See why I told you to buckle up?!

It is the end of human history as we know it and the beginning of our glorious unending— the eternal state (Rev. 21:1-5).

Yes! The new heaven and new earth are ushered in!

Now get back in your imaginary seat in our imaginary theatre.

The curtain opens.

You see him or her—the artist, author, entertainer, the person you wrote earlier—and your heart leaps. You are here for this moment. But then something happens.

You are invited on stage. The person you longed to see calls you by name and says, "I'm here for you. Come with me. I want to spend time with you."

How would that make you feel?

Okay, can I just say if I were sitting in the Encore Theatre in Las Vegas and Lionel Ritchie said something like that when he took the stage, I would fall over and freak out. But he would say it like this: "Jennifer, hello. Is it me you're looking for? Well, I'm stuck on you because you're three times a lady, so let's sail on."

Or if I were at Magdalen College Oxford in a grand lecture hall and C. S. Lewis stepped behind the lectern, with his booming British vibe he'd intone: "Jennifer, I know there's a problem of pain, but you are about to be surprised by joy, so come out of the silent planet."

Hahaha!

Okay, sorry if that was dumb.

But you get the idea. You showed up for the person behind the curtain, just to find out he or she showed up for you.

Showed. Up. For. You.

That is what happens when Jesus returns and we inhabit the new earth with Him.

Just for fun, tell me who is behind that curtain! For me, it was C. S. Lewis and Lionel. Who is it for you and why? Let me know on your favorite social media platform, using #HeavenStudy

But that's not even the best part. Imagine yourself on that stage one last time. Hear that person you came to see call your name, then, look around. Tune in. Do you see them? Can you hear their names also? The beautiful thing is that this moment, though so individual and personal, is also for every person who was waiting for this appearance.

When Jesus returns, He comes for you, and that is because He comes for all of us, His Bride, the church. All of us. We'll talk more about this in a few days, but for now, I just want to right size that stage in your imagination! The spotlight isn't on you or me. The spotlight is on Jesus and the invitation is for His bride, the church, all of us who are in Christ. We will all step onto that "stage" because it is as vast and inviting as the heart of God.

Jesus came the first time to Bethlehem for us. Jesus will come again for us. He returns for us, His brothers and sisters, His joint heirs, His family (Rom. 8:16-17; Gal. 3:29).

Read **Revelation 21:3-5** again.

So beautiful, right?

Rewrite those verses using personal pronouns and your name. Rephrase the verses to capture the idea of God's invitation and our expectation to be together forever.

Oh, my friend, God's very dwelling will be with you. He will be your God; you will be His girl. All the old will be gone. God will make it all new.

So, this week we'll leave our imaginary seats in the theatre, step onto the stage with the One our souls love and walk with Him into our forever home on the new earth, which is our forever Heaven.

All right, see you tomorrow. And plan to travel light; there are some old earth things you won't need on the new earth!

Good job today.

The No Mores

"God washes the eyes by tears until they can behold the invisible land where tears shall come no more."[2]

HENRY WARD BEECHER

We're finally here. Our eternal home. Together. Sporting our resurrected bodies! Oh, girl, you look good!

Welcome home.

Now that we're on the new earth, be prepared. There are a few things you were used to that are no more.

> **Read Revelation 21:4** and list the things that will be missing. (I guarantee you will not miss them!)
>
> 1. _____
> 2. _____
> 3. _____
> 4. _____

Lord, thank You for making death, mourning, crying, and pain no more someday. May the truth of our forever days on the new earth encourage us today as You prepare our hearts for Heaven. Amen (1 Thess. 4:17-18).

NO MORE DEATH, GRIEF, CRYING, PAIN

Focus on the end of **Revelation 21:4**. What reason is given for God wiping away tears and establishing this beautiful list of "no mores"?

Death, mourning, crying, and pain will be no more because the old order of things has passed away. Those are old earth things, not new earth things.

Read **Isaiah 25:6-9** and put in your own words how the prophet Isaiah described this day.

Thousands of years ago, Isaiah prophesied about a celebratory event that will take place between God and His people. The event will include a feast, the destruction of death, and God wiping tears from the eyes of the saints. The imagery and application fit the new earth.

If our forever Heaven is a place of no crying, why might you show up with tears? What could they be from? What might they represent?

Perhaps tears are the shadow of earth's sorrow. Perhaps our tears reflect where we've been, what we've felt, what we've endured. Death. Sorrow. Mourning. Pain. All these evoke tears. Perhaps the final wiping away of tears is an opportunity for us to really know, understand, and be assured that the old order is over.

Behold, all things have become new.

I wonder, could it be that God lets us show up in Heaven with a few lingering tears just so we can feel His tender and compassionate touch as He wipes them away?

> Now put yourself in your forever home on the new earth. What kinds of thoughts and emotions does **Revelation 7:15–17** evoke when it comes to tears in Heaven?

What a tender, heart-rending picture of God's kind compassion as He brushes away the tears on your cheeks. It is intimate and sheltering. In some ways it feels to me like both a final and a first all at once, a "that was then, this is now" moment. Not only will we shed no more tears, but we will also enter into such a closeness and intimacy with God that we will feel sheltered and cared for. Perhaps you need to feel that way today. Oh, my sister, that ultimate longing will be fulfilled when our faith becomes sight, but you can still know the safety of the Lamb of God as your Shepherd even now.

> Look again at **Isaiah 25:9**.
>
> Rewrite that verse and make it about this day, not just that day. And rephrase it as a prayer affirmation to the Lord, not just about Him.

Here's mine: *I will say on this day, behold, this is my God; You are our God! I have trusted in You and waited for You; we have all trusted and waited for You. You have saved us and will save us. We have all anticipated, longed for, and expected You. I am glad. We are glad. We are overwhelmed and full of joy because of You, because You are our salvation and shelter on this very day.*

Oh, friend, can you even imagine that kind of confidence, comfort, and companionship? This is our God, and this is our future.

NO MORE NIGHT

Read **Revelation 21:23-25; 22:5**. After you read those verses, put down your pen and close your eyes for a moment. Contemplate the darkness of night. Note the emotions you experience. Notice how the darkness limits you. Then consider: on the new earth, darkness doesn't exist.

Think for a moment: what does darkness typically represent in Scripture, literature, and cultural lingo?

The apostle Paul used darkness to symbolize sin and spiritual ignorance in Ephesians 5:8-12. Shakespeare used darkness to represent evil in his play Macbeth (Act One, Scene Five). Even in current lingo, people say, "I'm in the dark," which means they have no knowledge.

What does light typically represent in Scripture, literature, and current lingo?

David used light to represent how God's Word gives guidance in Psalm 119:105. Plato used light to symbolize knowledge or enlightenment in his allegory of the cave. And in current culture people say, "I saw the light," and it means they came to a moment of realization or understanding.

Now that you've thought about all that, read **Revelation 22:5** again and describe what the new earth, our forever Heaven, will be like using the representative and symbolic meanings of night and day, darkness and light.

There will be no more sin or effects of sin. You will be presented faultless before God's throne (Jude 24-25). There will be no more spiritual ignorance because you will know as you are known (1 Cor. 13:12). You will walk in the light as He is in the light and will have fellowship with everyone you encounter (1 John 1:7). There will be no more groping or grasping because the glory of God and the Lamb will be your light (Rev. 21:23; 22:5).

Oh, can I just say: I cannot wait! I long for that day, that city, that light! Sure, some of my excited anticipation is because of my blindness. I will walk in the light with no white cane ever again! But also, it's the freedom from sin and the comfort of being known, and it's the absolute mind-blowing anticipation of having nothing to separate me from the One my soul loves. Oh, thank You, Jesus, our risen Lamb, Light of the world.

NO MORE TEMPLE

Flip back to **Revelation 21:22** for this last "no more." Why did John say he didn't see a temple?

The Lord God Almighty and the Lamb are the temple on the new earth.

What does that even mean?

To find out, let's think about the original purpose of the temple.

Read **1 Kings 8:6-20** for a hint.

The temple was the place God's presence dwelt among His people. Yet, when His people were scattered in exile with no access to the temple, how beautiful that God's presence became for His people a temple of sorts, a sanctuary (Ezek. 11:16).

Based on what you've read in **Revelation 21–22**, (especially 21:3), why does there not need to be a temple in our forever home of the new earth?

Even though God connected with His people through the temple, by its design the structure kept the people distant from God and separate from each other. The Gentiles could only be in the outer court. Jewish women could get a little closer in the court of women, but not much. Jewish men inched up a little further into the court of Israel. The priests could almost get into God's presence in the holy place. And just once a year the high priest could enter the most holy place, the holy of holies.

The temple layout was like a physical picture of how distant humanity still was from God. It makes sense. Humanity is sinful. God is holy. And though now we have access to God through the work of Christ and the Holy Spirit in us, we are still physically limited from being fully in His presence. But one day, in our new resurrection bodies, that will not be the case. There will be no need for a temple because the new heaven and new earth will be God's holy of holies and we, His holy people, will be in His presence and He will dwell among us.

Oh, my. Pardon me while I shout "Hallelujah!"

But my friend, don't miss the blessing of Heaven by waiting for that day alone to experience His presence and His promise.

When you are in Christ, through His Spirit, He abides with you right now. You are the temple of His Spirit; you are in Him, and He is in you. He is light, and in Him is no darkness at all. His dwelling is with you. As you hide His Word in your heart, His light guides you.

Now, be the temple and walk in the light! Boom! Yes!

Done for today!

DAY 3

The No Longers

"Heaven gives us hope and makes our present burdens easier to bear."[3]

BILLY GRAHAM

Get your sunscreen. You're getting a tour of some of my favorite beaches.

I grew up near Clearwater Beach. I loved kicking up the sand along the shore and feeling the power of the ocean. A bit later, my parents were missionaries in Costa Rica. I have such fond memories of splashing in Puntarenas on the Pacific coast and making castles in that fine, golden sand near the shore.

Then as a teenager, we lived in Miami. Lots of Saturdays I'd be slathered in baby oil, laying out on the beach, listening to Lionel Ritchie and the crashing of Atlantic waves. (I know, I know. Don't email me. Baby oil is the worst thing you can put on your skin, and sunbathing isn't very smart either! I was young and ignorant!) Moving on.

In West Palm Beach as a college student and later as a young wife, I often walked hand-in-hand with Phil across the bridge to the ocean where we'd sit on the seawall and talk and dream.

And at the present moment, I'm not standing at my glass-top white desk at home. I'm sitting outside overlooking the harbor in Treasure Island, Florida. I feel the breeze, hear the call of pelicans and the distant waves. It's so restorative.

You got the theme here, right? I love the water!

> What about you? Are you a beach girl? Or maybe a lake girl? Or maybe it's the mountains you love? What location or part of nature brings you a sense of joy and restores your soul when you're there? Why?

It's hard to imagine our forever home on the new earth without the restored creation of those places we love, isn't it? Well, hold that thought.

Lord, as we meditate upon Your Word today, make us wise. Amen (Ps. 119:99).

Skim through **Revelation 21**. Don't do a thorough study, just a quick skim.

Write out a description of what this city, our eternal home, is like. (You don't need to be overly specific. Just communicate the ideas and think like a marketer!)

If I were a realtor, here's what I would post to try to get folks to want to move in.

> This beautiful city is known by those who belong there as the new Jerusalem. It's been compared to the splendor of a radiant bride on her wedding day. God Himself is everywhere with everyone all the time. Yes, God. The One you're thinking about. Yahweh. Wow, right?
>
> No one cries, because God made everything new in this place. There is no evil. The city is like none other because it descended from Heaven itself. It sparkles like precious stones. The walls and gates are splendid. Yet, full disclosure: there is no sea.

Whaaat?

That last statement might lose me a few clients! Paradise with no sea (Rev. 21:1)?

NO LONGER A SEA

If you love to walk by the ocean, you may think Heaven can't be Heaven without your happy place. What does the Bible mean? Is this literal or metaphor?

To figure this out, let's start by reading **Genesis 1:1-3**.

This is literal water. Yet what might the water also represent in the creation account?

Disorder and darkness. In ancient thought, the sea represented tumult, danger, turmoil, and chaos. In fact, a well-known Canaanite myth depicted the sea as a monstrous beast and a place where Baal would battle with Yam, the sea god.

Spooky!

Read **Psalm 69:1-3**; **Psalm 124:1-5**. What's the view of water in these verses?

Water was perceived as dangerous and threatening. It was more powerful than human ability to control or overcome. The sea was perceived as a place of terror and chaos, an abyss of hopelessness and isolation. Only God was more powerful than the sea (Ps. 93:4).

So, again I ask, are John's words about the abolition of the sea literal or symbolic?

Hmmm, maybe both?

Jesus told us in Matthew 22:30 that there would be no marriage in our forever home. Remember? In context, that should be taken literally. Yet, it also has a symbolic truth associated with it. (Go back to pp. 118–119 to review.)

Marriage is an earthly need-meeter, and on the new earth we will not have the same needs. So perhaps the lack of sea on the new earth is literal as well as symbolic.

If you have access to a globe, glance at it. Otherwise, think back to fourth grade when your teacher had one on her desk. Do the oceans join or separate the land masses?

Yep, seas separate us. We'll talk more tomorrow about how we will be one unified community on the new earth. Perhaps there is no sea because there is no division among us. Perhaps there is no need for a salty sea because we will be nourished and sustained by something better.

> How does **Revelation 22:1-5** support that we will no longer have or need a sea?

The water of life will constantly flow from the throne down the middle of the city. Crystal clear. This too could be literal and symbolic. (See Isa. 12:3; Joel 3:18; John 7:38.)

Remember, metaphor and symbolism are pointers. They point to deeper truth. Sometimes we need imagery to draw a picture our hearts understand even if we can't totally explain it in our heads.

> Pause here and read **Psalm 46**.

> See in your mind's eye the rich imagery used to symbolize not just your future hope, but your present confidence. Pray the psalm back to God and linger here as long as you want. I'll wait.

> "The LORD sits enthroned over the flood. The LORD sits enthroned, King forever. The LORD gives his people strength. The LORD blesses his people with peace."

> **PSALM 29:10-11 (CSB)**

NO LONGER A CURSE

> Read **Revelation 22:3** again for the last "no longer."

> What curse is the Bible talking about here? (See Gen. 2:16-17; 3:14-19.)

The curse that was initiated back in the garden brought toil and pain and suffering upon us and our world. It was a curse brought on by sin. And sin brings with it the curse of death. And that death sentence gets applied to everyone and everything.

> What are some examples of sin's effect in your life and the world around you?

You don't have to look far to see the effects of the curse. Just look outside your window. The ground itself feels the curse; thorns and thistles make it hard to produce. The animal kingdom feels the curse. The lion does not lay down with the lamb. We see ripples of the curse in our relationships, our work, our government—all things in our world.

But it won't always be this way!

There will be a day when we are raised to move into the new earth. All effects of the curse will be eradicated.

> We're all waiting for this. How does **Romans 8:19-23** confirm this longing?

Yep, I groan. You groan. All God's children groan! The trees in your backyard, the forest and the fields, the mountains and streams, all nature groans because all feel the effects of the curse. But it's not forever!

> Look again at **Isaiah 11:6-9** and read **Isaiah 32:15-18**. Use a few adjectives to describe how these verses illustrate this post-curse land and life.

Verdant. Fertile. Just. Peaceful. Right.

Can't you just see it? It will be beautiful. Eden restored. Blue flowers everywhere. Animals will hang out together with no need to worry that Fido may be Smokey the Bear's dinner! And if you're a gardener, imagine this day while you're currently sweating and pulling weeds. The curse will be broken! No weeds!

> And look what else happens in **Revelation 14:13**.

We will rest from our labor. Some of you are like, *Whew! That is a curse I want broken! I can finally retire or quit this dead-end job.* And for others, like me, we're not sure how we feel about this. I like to be productive, industrious, and I feel most alive when I am working on or at something.

Is labor part of the curse that will be lifted?

If there is no labor on the new earth, will we be bored out of our minds?

> Let's pop back into Eden for a sec. How does **Genesis 3:17–19** describe the result of Adam's original sin?

Ouch. The ground was cursed. Ever since, it has been uncooperative and requires "painful toil." But prior to Adam's sin and the curse, it was Adam's job to cultivate the garden (Gen. 2:15).

We have no idea what the pre-fall ecology was like, but we can imagine that working the garden required a little human creativity, exertion, and intellect to pull it off. It was virtuous, God-ordained work.

If the new earth is a restored and renewed Eden, "the consummation of all that Eden intended to be," then it makes sense for there to be purposeful work to do there.[4] Yet the Bible said we would rest from our labor.

So, what gives?

> Find the Greek word for *labor* in **Revelation 14:13** using your favorite
> Bible resource (like blueletterbible.org) or an internet search. Write the
> word and what it means.

Kopos is the word for *labor*, and it speaks of toil and fatigue. It's a picture of intense effort; it's hard and troubling. It can also denote sorrow.

> Based on what you know about our eternal state, does that kind of labor sound like it fits on the new earth? Explain.

I don't think so either! It seems we will get rest from *kopos* and instead get the joy of working in the way God originally intended before the fall—work that serves God, His creation, each other, and satisfies us deeply. Ultimately, our work will serve the One who sits on the throne, the One who shelters us with His presence (Rev. 7:15; 22:3).

> What are your thoughts about this? Do you look forward to work on the new earth? What kind of work? There is no wrong answer here. Just apply your biblically informed imagination and dream big!

I have so many things I want to learn and do! But deep down, I just want to serve. Now, don't think I'm being super spiritual or weird here, but with blindness, people always have to serve me. And I am so thankful, but I wish it weren't always that way. I would love to look over and notice when your teacup needs to be topped off, then jump up and fill it before you even ask. I would love to drive my mom to an appointment or clean out her fridge or weed her garden. I would love to do a million things for my husband, who is always serving me in the most practical behind-the-scenes ways. I miss serving in those physical, tangible ways that help people.

I understand God has given me other ways to serve. But I'm just saying, in Christ, we are wired to serve (Mark 10:45). And when we finally get there to our eternal home, watch out. I am going to out-serve you if I can! I can't wait to work with all I've got for the glory of God and the good of His people.

Can you even imagine such a lovely kind of labor? It is rest. It is work without the strain of sin. It is how a God-centered, God-honoring community will function.

That is work without the curse.

So, what if you bring a little bit of that Heaven to all you do here and now? What if you serve knowing you are sheltered by the presence of the One who sits on the throne? What if you ask God to make your work produced by faith and your labor prompted by love (1 Thess. 1:3)? How might that change your current work and become an answer to Jesus's prayer in **Matthew 6:10**?

Lord, You are worthy of our work here. May Your kingdom come and Your will be done here on earth as it is and will be in Heaven. May we serve You and each other with our whole selves. Amen.

All right, we're wrapping up for now. So let me leave you with this. Our forever Heaven reminds us that Jesus once and forever conquered all evil, division, turmoil, and chaos. He has broken the curse, making all things new.

The next time you see a raging sea, remember, Jesus can walk on that. The next time tidal waves of stress threaten or you feel like you're drowning in your own ocean of salty tears, remember He has authority over the billows and crashing waves. He replaces that sea with a river of life.

We will see that fully consummated in our forever Heaven. But when you are in Christ, He does that in your heart even now. He didn't save you just to bring you to Heaven someday; He saved you to bring Heaven to you on this day. Heaven is peace. Heaven is a river of life flowing from His throne. Heaven is the presence of Christ.

"Instead, you have come to Mount Zion, to the city of the living God (the heavenly Jerusalem), to myriads of angels, a festive gathering, to the assembly of the firstborn whose names have been written in heaven, to a Judge, who is God of all, to the spirits of righteous people made perfect."

HEBREWS 12:22-23 (CSB)

Whew! Good stuff! Tomorrow you'll get to meet those you'll spend your forever with.

DAY 4
Every Nation, Tribe, and Tongue

"Believers are never told to become one;
we already are one and are expected to act like it."[5]

JONI EARECKSON TADA

Hey there! We're almost fully moved into the new earth, and today we'll meet the neighbors! I hope you're studying in a place that awakens your imagination and stirs your senses. I'm sitting at my white glass-top desk, enjoying the fragrance of a blue flower candle. And fun fact—I made it!

Now, don't ask me for one. It's not pretty! With blindness, my pour isn't very even. But girl, I'm really good at scent creation! Ha! It's blue hydrangea and throws a sweet, intense, almost fruity scent. I used a wood wick, so it crackles and sputters, serenading me while I type.

You remember the reason for my blue flower candle, right?

In literature the blue flower represents longing. It symbolizes a desire, yearning, and love of the eternal. And at this point in our study of Heaven, seeds of the blue flower are blossoming all over the landscape of my imagination. My heart is so attached to Heaven and most of all, to the treasure of Heaven, Jesus. I long for that day when our faith becomes sight.

I love imagining our forever home on the new earth, carpeted with blue flowers.

Lord, open the eyes of our hearts so we can see clearly the hope You have called us to and the riches we have in the inheritance of each other. Amen (Eph. 1:18).

This week we've seen that the new earth, our forever Heaven, is like a renewed and restored garden of Eden with no temple, sea, pain, sorrow, tears, and curse. But today I want us to take another look through John's lens at the new earth to see who is there.

Turn to **Revelation 21** and jot down what John saw (or didn't see) in the following verses:

Verse 1

Verse 2

Verse 22

Yep, we saw some stunning real estate and the absence of some artifacts, but where are the people?

Look at **Revelation 7:9** and record what John saw.

Every nation, tribe, people, and language. All gathered, one redeemed collective.

What is the significance of John pointing out the variety of redeemed souls who were gathered?

They were one collective composed of many different people groups, cultures, and nationalities. They were unique, yet they were unified.

I don't need to tell you that a shadow of the curse still darkening our world today is division.

It manifests in racism, prejudice against ethnic groups, apartheid, genocide, and all sorts of other forms of "us vs. them." It may be based on ignorance or fear or evil or hatred. But no matter the human basis, it is all a result of the curse of sin and death that divides and kills. When Adam and Eve fell to sin in the garden, we all fell into the trap of pride and fear that divides, and we've been there ever since.

Look back all the way to **Genesis 11:1-9**.

What did the people say they wanted to do, and why (v. 4)?

They wanted to build a city to make a name for themselves so they wouldn't be scattered.

What was the result of their effort? (vv. 8-9)?

Different languages, dispersion, division. They didn't get the city, and they didn't get the name they wanted. They got what we're still dealing with today: differences that divide.

Let me be clear: it is not a curse or result of the curse to be of different cultures, skin colors, nationalities, and languages. The diversity reflects God's creative intent. But the division created by the way our pride and fear respond to those differences is a result of the curse. You don't have to look far to see how easily humans "other" other humans who differ from them to establish their own territory and protect their own name.

But listen; do you hear it? The forever Heaven of the new earth shouts back to Babel the redemption and renewal that God has planned. There is a whisper of that redemption and renewal taking place now. It started at Pentecost with the coming of the Holy Spirit and the spreading of the gospel from Jerusalem, to Judea, to Samaria and to the uttermost parts of the earth—the good news reaching to all nations. But the culminating cry is still to come. Get quiet and tune your heart to hear. Can you hear the echo of truth resounding from the new earth? *This is the city, the home you long for. Everything else was a shadow, a shallow substitute for this—the city where your God dwells and you find your true name!*

Read the following passages aloud in the order listed:
Hebrews 11:10; 13:14; and **Revelation 21:2**. Journal any thoughts you have after reading about our coming city.

Back in the days of Babel, we humans longed for a city. It didn't end well. But God, in removing the curse, redeems that longing and builds us a city where every nation, every tribe, every tongue shows up as one in Him. Hallelujah! Amen.

Now read **Revelation 7:9** again. What modifiers or qualifiers come before the words *tribe, nation,* etc.?

This is kind of a trick question! We might say no qualifiers are there, but look again, the word *every* IS a qualifier. All people will be represented. However, the Bible doesn't tell us we will be formerly of a specific tribe or once from a particular nation. Our oneness will exist, yet so will our uniqueness. We will not have our cultures, nationalities, languages, or differences erased, but the city will be enhanced by every ethnicity, skin color, language, culture, and tribe. What we will have in common is our new earth DNA and our holiness in Christ.

Why do you think it matters to God to preserve our tribal, cultural, and national identities?

Author Richard Mouw wrote: "There is no one human individual or group who can fully bear or manifest all that is involved in the image of God, so that there is a sense in which that image is collectively possessed. The image of God is, as it were, parceled out among the peoples of the earth. By looking at different individuals and groups, we get glimpses of different aspects of the full image of God."[6]

You are complete in Christ and are created to bear and reflect His image. So am I. So is every single human on this planet. Though our individuality completely bears His image, perhaps the nations, tribes, and cultures are specifically mentioned in the new earth because God's beautiful image is also captured corporately. His essence and character and image are so vast and deep and lovely that the collective of His creation reflects His multi-faceted beauty.

Now read **Revelation 21:24–26** again and describe the contribution each nation and tribe make to our forever home on the new earth.

Use your biblically informed imagination to envision what it could look like in a practical way for the nations and tribes to bring their splendor, glory, and honor into the new Jerusalem. Consider the strengths and contributions of the nations and cultures you have visited or know about.

Personally, I think of the kindness of the Filipinos. I marvel at the charm of the British. I love the exuberance of people I've met from various African countries. And Italy? Ohh, the food. The music. The fragrances.

The skills, culture, and way of life of every single nation and people group are all part of the glory and honor that will be brought into the new Jerusalem. All God's creatures and creation reflect Him as our creative Creator. And the borrowed glory each will bring into the city will reflect and affirm God's glory in creation.

But here is an interesting thought. What did we not see in John's vision of every tribe, culture, and people group from **Revelation 7:9**?

John never mentioned any individuals. Hmm.

In Eden, humanity was represented by two people: Adam and Eve. But not in the restored, renewed garden, the new earth. John's vision was bigger. It was corporate in nature. God's restoration and redemption is for the whole earth, all of creation and people from every tribe, culture, and language. And how will they get there? God does this as we, the church, carry out the Great Commission to go and make disciples of ALL NATIONS. The beautiful diversity will be there because the church is completing her mission.

You are redeemed and will be raised, restored, and fully alive in your resurrection body. But it's not going to be just you and Jesus. Heaven is a team sport! It will be as intimate as you alone with your Shepherd, yet as immersive and integrated as a flock, all being fed and led by their Shepherd—all of us together.

Jesus's body was broken on the cross on that dark day so we would be whole—one body, His people forever on the new earth (Rev. 5:9).

> All right, glance back to Babel one last time (Gen. 11). They wanted to make a name for themselves, didn't they? Well, read how God meets that longing in that city in **Revelation 2:17**. Draw a sketch of it and think about what could be written on the stone.

The white stone with a new name is truly a mystery, and scholars have many different views on what this could mean. But one of my favorite possibilities is this: there was an ancient Roman tradition where the victorious athlete was awarded a white stone bearing his name when he won a competition. This white stone served as a ticket to an award banquet.

If this meaning holds true, you can see how and why you get the equivalent of a white stone with a new name when you move into that city. He gives you honor and entrance into your forever reward of the forever Heaven.

A new name is great and all, but what is even better is another name—the Name.

Read **Revelation 22:4** and just pause and imagine that beautiful experience.

We will see His face, and His name will be on our foreheads.

Listen to my conversation with Derwin Gray about healing racial division at **413podcast.com/207**.

Oh, Jesus, Lamb of God, King of Heaven, thank You for making us Yours and giving us Your name. We are honored and humbled to be called Yours.

May we wear His name well. Love like He loves, live like He lived, and serve like He served.

Yes and amen.

Good job!

This week is a wrap. Tomorrow you're going to do some *Dash Living*. And in the video teaching, you'll take a seat at the marriage supper of the Lamb.

But review those *Takeaway Truths* first!

TAKEAWAY TRUTHS

Below are some important points we covered this week. There's also room for you to add other takeaways you want to remember.

- There are various end times views, but they all include the return of Christ, final judgment, and the inauguration of the new heavens and new earth. End times views are not a primary issue, and agreement with a certain view should not be a test of fellowship in the body of Christ.

- Some things that are unfortunately commonplace in our human experience on earth—death, grief, crying, pain—will not be part of our eternal existence on the new earth. They will be gone forever.

- Darkness and the deeds of darkness will not exist in the new heavens and new earth. The glory of God through the light of Christ will be our illumination for all eternity. Neither will there be need for a temple or anything else that represents the presence of God in the new earth because He will be with us.

- Sorry beach lovers, no more sea in the new heavens and new earth. In Scripture the sea represented chaos and disorder. Those won't exist in the new heavens and new earth. Plus, the sea is presently a separator. There will be no separation for believers on the new earth.

- On the new earth, the ancient curse that has affected all of life will no longer be in effect. We will enjoy sinless living and joyful work for the King.

IMAGINE YOUR FUTURE

On this *Dash Living Day*, contemplate, imagine, and put in writing what you think it will be like when you get to Heaven (both the current Heaven and life on the new earth).

Describe in first person and present tense what your thoughts, emotions, and experience might be based on your biblically informed imagination. This will help you grow more deeply attached to the reality of Heaven and provide comfort to the ones you love who will read these words once you are there.

"Therefore my heart is glad and my whole being rejoices; my body also rests securely. For you will not abandon me to Sheol; you will not allow your faithful one to see decay. You reveal the path of life to me; in your presence is abundant joy. At your right hand are eternal pleasures."

PSALM 16:9-11 (CSB)

CELEBRATING AT THE TABLE

BEFORE THE VIDEO

Welcome and Prayer

WATCH THE VIDEO

FOUR TABLES:

1. **Table of** _____ (Exodus 25)

   • Remember: _____

2. **The** _____ **table** (Psalm 23)

   • Remember: _____

3. **The** _____ **table** (Matthew 26)

   • Remember: _____

Any table we sit at gives us an _____ to anticipate the table that is to _____.

4. **The marriage supper of the** _____ (Revelation 19)

THREE PARTS OF THE JEWISH WEDDING TRADITION:

1. **Sign the** _____

2. **Here comes the** _____

3. **The** _____ **supper**

Our time on the new earth will not just be _____; it will be _____.

To access the video teaching sessions, use the instructions in the back of your Bible study book.

CONVERSATION GUIDE

PERSONAL BIBLE STUDY

- What was your favorite day of study? Why?

- What are your thoughts and emotions as you consider the return of Christ, the judgment, and taking up residence in the new earth?

- What is something painful or difficult you've faced or are currently facing that you will no longer have to deal with in our forever home? Express the joy that reality brings you!

- Which "no longer" or "no more" resonates most with you and why?

- What's the significance of John pointing out the variety of redeemed people gathered in Heaven? And what's significant about God preserving our tribal, cultural, and national identities?

- Which *Takeaway Truth* stands out to you and why?

- *Dash Living Day*: Based on your biblically informed imagination, describe some of what you think it will be like when you get to Heaven.

VIDEO TEACHING

- What's one thing that stood out to you from the video teaching? Why?

- Which of the three tables (showbread, Shepherd, Last Supper) revealed Jesus to you in a surprising or meaningful way? Explain.

- How does any table we sit at provide an opportunity to anticipate the wedding feast to come? Are you taking advantage of those opportunities? If so, in what way? If not, what can you do to make every table a pointer to the marriage supper table?

- Which part of the Jewish wedding tradition meant the most to you and why?

- How does the marriage supper of the Lamb mark the fulfillment of God's redemptive plan? Describe what the union of Jesus the Lamb with His bride, the church, means to you.

SESSION SIX

"Since, then, you have been raised with Christ, set your hearts on things above, where Christ is, seated at the right hand of God. Set your minds on things above, not on earthly things. For you died, and your life is now hidden with Christ in God. When Christ, who is your life, appears, then you also will appear with him in glory."

COLOSSIANS 3:1-4

SET YOUR MIND ON THINGS ABOVE

After five weeks of having Heaven in our hearts and in our heads, we will focus on how it impacts our hands, feet, and lives here on earth. The "someday" of Heaven should make a difference on this day.

We'll see how Scripture gives us all we need to navigate this world that's not really our home. As sojourners on earth, with our citizenship in Heaven, we will get practical strategies for seeking and setting our minds on things above. We'll understand the impact of living in the "already and not yet" and how we best live in this time. On the last day of this study, we will candidly discuss what it looks like to live well and die well in light of our heavenly reality. This week will challenge us to live out the hope of Heaven so that God's will is done "on earth as it is in Heaven."

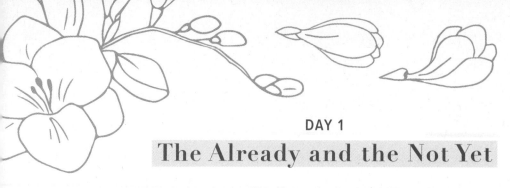

The Already and the Not Yet

"My Heaven born faith gives promise of eternal sight.
My new birth, a pledge of never-ending life."[1]

THE VALLEY OF VISION

We've made it to the last week of our study together! Aren't you so grateful for what you've learned, and maybe, unlearned so far? Me too.

Hopefully you have an increased longing for Heaven, and more importantly, the treasure of Heaven, Jesus. So, get comfy, get your coffee or whatever you enjoy sipping while you study, and let's get going.

> *Make us to know Your ways, Lord. Teach us Your paths. Lead us in Your truth. We want to be learners today. You are the God who saves us and we trust You. Amen (Ps. 25:4-5).*

Since we have all slept a bit since we started this thing, let's review. There is a present Heaven where we go when we die. We refer to it as the intermediate state where we will rest fully alive in His presence in our Father's house. We've noted that God has placed eternity in our hearts—an awareness, ache, and anticipation for our eternal home and our eternal life through Christ.

We've affirmed that Jesus Christ will return one day, and we who are in Christ will be raised in an imperishable and incorruptible resurrection body and will inhabit the new earth together with Him forever. We've grappled with hard questions about Heaven and concluded that our deepest satisfaction doesn't come from answers about Heaven but instead from a relationship with the God of Heaven.

Then last week we saw the stunning images, both physical and symbolic of our forever home on the new earth, where every tribe and tongue will worship Jesus and thrive in our restored Eden. So, what in the world is left to talk about?

If most of what we've discussed is in our future (the "not yet"), then what about now? What if I told you that what is "not yet" is also an "already"?

Here's what I mean.

> Read 1 John 3:2.
>
> What is the "now" in this verse?
>
>
>
>
> What is the "not yet"?

We are God's children now. But we don't know yet what we will fully be, except that we will be like Him.

> Now look at what the Bible says about the now you.
>
> Romans 8:30: Who or what are you?
>
>
>
>
> Ephesians 2:6: Who or what are you now?

You are glorified and seated in the heavenly realms. Yep, that's you. Wearing your worn-out jeans, with messy hair, sitting at your kitchen table in that squeaky chair! Really? I don't feel very glorious. And last I checked, my bottom is seated in my white fuzzy desk chair!

And what gives us the right to be sitting in such a high and holy place? Because Christ is. We are raised up with Him and seated with Him because we are in Christ Jesus.

Hmmm, let's keep going.

Look up the following references and fill out the Now/Not Yet chart:

NOW	NOT YET
Romans 8:15-16 I am:	**Romans 8:23** I am not yet:
Ephesians 1:7 I am (have):	**Ephesians 4:30** I am (have) not yet (received):
Luke 11:20 What has already come?	**Luke 17:20** What is not yet observable?

You are adopted in Christ. Yet, not yet adopted.

You are already redeemed, but not yet fully redeemed.

The kingdom of God has come, yet the kingdom of God isn't yet observable.

The list goes on . . .

And all the seeming contradictions are absolutely true by themselves and together.

So how can this already and not yet both be true? What do you think?

We live in the gap between Jesus's two comings, the time between the already and the not yet. Bible scholars call this concept *inaugurated eschatology* or *kingdom theology*.

If you're ambitious, look up and write definitions for both of those phrases:

Inaugurated eschatology says the kingdom of God is here, beginning at the first coming of Jesus, but it will not be fully consummated until Christ's second coming.

Here's my simplified take: The kingdom of Heaven has come and is yet to come.

You've probably seen the phrases "kingdom of Heaven" and "kingdom of God" in the New Testament. Here's a little clarification.

Both phrases refer to the same thing. Matthew, in his Gospel, uses the phrase "kingdom of Heaven," while Mark and Luke use the phrase "kingdom of God." The two phrases are interchangeable.

As Christians, we are part of and involved in the kingdom of God/Heaven here and now, yet God's kingdom hasn't and won't come to its ultimate fulfillment until Christ returns.

God's kingdom is both present and future all at once. Jesus reigns, and Jesus will reign. He came, and He will come. You are raised, and you will be raised. You are redeemed and adopted, yet you will also be redeemed and adopted.

Now and not yet. Get it?

I remember when I was expecting our first son, Clayton, I was so tuned into every moment. That tiny human was already a baby the moment he was conceived—even before I knew he was growing within me. He didn't become more of a human baby once I felt the first kick or once he finally left the womb. (Which, by the way, took way too long; and why didn't some nice older woman say, "Honey, no matter what it costs, get an epidural!")

Clayton was a baby all along. He was here, but not yet here. But finally, on October 10, the fullness of the reality could be seen, touched, and grasped. I think the already and not yets of the kingdom of Heaven are like that.

This waiting for final realization is why we live by faith, not by sight. And the already and not yet affirms our faith will become sight.

Oh, my friend, your heavenly status is now, you don't have to wait and wish, as if it is only a not yet. You can treat it as the already it is now!

> Maybe that's what Paul is helping us do in **Colossians 3:1–4**.
>
> Read those verses and list what Paul told us to do specifically in verses 1 and 2.
>
> **Verse 1** Because I am raised with Christ, I can _____
> _____
>
> **Verse 2** I can _____

You can seek the things above ("set your mind on," NIV) and set your mind on things above rather than earthly things. But how?

TWO GREEK WORDS

Zeteo is the Greek word in Colossians 3:1 translated *seek* or *keep seeking*, and it means to seek with the intention of finding. It can also mean to crave something.[2]

Ooh, I get that concept. Do you?

All I have to say to explain it is one word: chocolate. Okay, two words: dark chocolate.

> If you experience food cravings, what do you typically crave?
>
>
>
> Have you ever looked for something valuable you lost or wanted to figure something out or desperately find something you want? Describe that kind of intense seeking.

I can be a pit bull when it comes to not letting go of a problem until I find the solution. I will seek until I find and wear out everyone around me who is watching me. There have been times when I craved dark chocolate so much that I've raided my pantry like an obsessed blind ninja just to find a half-eaten bag of stale chocolate chips!

To help you keep seeking and setting your mind on things above, memorize or meditate upon 2 Peter 1:3-11.

Paul was saying we need to seek heavenly things with that same intensity. A practical way I'm training myself to do this is by listening to Scripture on my phone. Instead of automatically turning on a fiction book (which is something I crave almost as much as dark chocolate), I'm developing a habit of Scripture listening. The more I do it, the more I want to do it.

You see, what might start as a discipline can turn into a delight. And what we delight in, we desire even more. You might practice "seeking" through listening to worship songs, playing an instrument, regularly praying with a friend, memorizing Scripture, or just practicing silence and meditation. You're making these kinds of choices over streaming videos or scrolling social media. You get the idea.

So, what can you do in a practical way to "keep seeking" things above? Jot down some ideas and choose one to practice for the next few days. Record your results and be ready to share those with your group or Bible study buddy.

My Ideas

The Results

Oh, my friend, we have been raised with Christ. That means we are identified with Christ and have been given new life through the power of the Holy Spirit. Thus, we can live a new way, God's way.[3] No living low and lesser. Let's not relentlessly seek things below—worldly things—when we can keep seeking things above.

Phroneo is the Greek word in Colossians 3:2 translated *set your mind*, and it describes a mindset or frame of mind. It is applied to how someone feels and thinks, especially their attitude concerning earthly things.[4]

Phroneo is also in the present tense. If you're a grammar girl, you get why that matters. It denotes continuous action. In other words, the command is to keep setting your mind. All the time, without ceasing, be a mind-setter!

Your mind is like ever-drying cement. You want to constantly think on things above so your eternal reality and hope gets cemented into your every thought and emotion. You want to set your mind on things above because what you dwell on creates neural pathways in your beautiful brain. Those pathways become mindsets which are revealed in our footsteps! In other words, thoughts lead to feelings and actions and habits.

We want our actions and decisions to be made with eternity in mind.

What are some "things above" thoughts you need to set your mind on? List a few, then pick one and (circle) it. Post it all over your home and recite it to yourself every day for the next few days. Note how the Holy Spirit changes your heart and attitude over time. Be ready to share your experience and results with your Bible study buddies.

Thoughts I need to set or reset:

The result of reciting a heavenly minded thought:
(Don't be discouraged if you haven't noticed a difference yet.
It takes at least fourteen days to develop a habit.)

Let's keep our thoughts cemented to Heaven and sticky noted to earth—it's how we live in this world in light of the world to come.

One important note: Being heavenly minded doesn't mean we disregard, dismiss, or diminish the earthly things we are called to steward—like our people, community, work, or calling. For the moment, we live in this world; we're just not of it. We get to be Christ's servants in it. What we invest our time, resources, and energies in is a good check on our heavenly mindedness. Are we invested in the old way of life that leads to death or the new way that brings life?

Good question to ponder.

That's enough for now. Good job!

See you tomorrow!

Go to **jenniferrothschild.com/heaven** to get my "7 Books on Heaven" reading list to help you go deeper and get even more excited about Heaven!

Develop a Sojourn Spirit

"I may live as a pilgrim in search of an eternal home, but I'll never end up on the far side of the sea alone. The voice that called me out is one with the hand that guides me. God's hand not only guides, it wraps around me, holding me fast, cradling me safe, and carrying me home."[5]

TINA BOESCH

I mentioned last week that my parents were missionaries near San Jose, Costa Rica. We lived in a borrowed house with a small backyard surrounded by a cement wall topped with broken glass to discourage would-be robbers. Evidently, this wasn't the safest part of town. In fact, the house was built with tiny windows high off the ground, again to deter thieves.

The only vulnerable spot in the house was a small jalousie window in the dining room that opened onto the carport. We didn't own a car, but the Catholic priest in the barrio did. He parked his car there, and we'd leave the light on at night to protect it.

Well, our home was one of the few with a car, so evidently word had gotten out that we had money.

One night my dad was awakened by a scratching, grinding sound coming from the dining room where the jalousie window was located. As he crept closer in the dark, he realized someone was removing each glass panel one by one. Dad's mind raced. What could he do? He had no weapon. He wasn't a citizen, so he had to be super smart and careful.

He prayed. He got an idea.

He left the dining room and slipped into my little brother's room where a putrid green rubber mask lay on the floor. Even now I can see that ugly thing with its oversized red eyes and electrified purple hair.

Dad pulled that mask over his head, tip-toed back to the dining room window and crouched beneath it. He listened until he heard the bad guys remove the last glass panel. Just then, with a hammering heart, my masked dad shot up, flung open the curtains, and screeched a monstrous primal scream!

The robbers screamed right back. They leaped backward with such force that they dented the priest's car and broke the glass panels stacked at their feet.

I have many memories from Costa Rica, but that one is my hands-down favorite!

During those years, we were sojourners in a foreign country. We remained American citizens. So, though we lived in Costa Rica and loved it, it was not our true home. America was.

That's how we need to think of earth now in light of Heaven. We live here, but this earth isn't our true home.

Lord, may Your Word be our lamp and light as we study. Amen (Ps. 119:105).

Read **Philippians 3:20**; **Hebrews 11:13**; and **1 Peter 2:11**.

How are believers described in these verses and what is our true homeland? (Read several translations to get a full picture.)

We're strangers, foreigners, exiles, and sojourners here on earth, because our true citizenship is in Heaven.

What does that mean to you?

Sometimes we need to pause and really consider our status. We live here on earth, and most of us probably love living here, and it feels like home. However, we need to remember it's not our true and ultimate home. We're sojourners here, and we need to live with a sojourner spirit, like the people in Hebrews 11.

Read **Hebrews 11:1-16**.

INDICATIONS OF A SOJOURN SPIRIT

1. Speak Sojourn

Reread **Hebrews 11:13** again. Notice the words *foreigners* and *strangers* (NIV).

Who called them that? Did the writer of Hebrews name them or was it the sojourning saints themselves?

They said it of themselves. They confessed they were strangers and exiles. Why does that matter?

Focus in on **Hebrews 11:14**. What does such speech affirm?

Their confession affirmed their true identity and their hearts' desire for a new homeland. They were citizens of a better country.

My friend, we too want to remember where our true citizenship is. That constant acknowledgement will not only affirm our identity, but confessing it frequently will affirm we know our true heavenly status—we live in the already and not yet. We want to live with a sojourn spirit, and speaking the language of sojourn can help us. Sometimes earth can feel long and heavy. Those are the days we need to speak sojourn!

You've probably heard me say, "earth is short; Heaven is long." That is my way of speaking sojourn! It realigns my heart, identity, and hope with who I am and what my true reality is. So, create some phrases or find Scriptures you can use to speak sojourn. You can borrow my "earth is short; Heaven is long" if you want! Another phrase I use is: "My citizenship is in Heaven." This really helps me when I feel out of place or insecure. And every time I feel stabs of grief, I speak, "Eden had no tombstones." I also often quote a line of

David Crowder's song, "Milk and Honey:" "I'm heading to a place where the flowers grow."[6] But of course, I include the word *blue* before *flowers* (wink!).

Make a list you can refer to when earth feels heavy and long.

My Speak Sojourn Ideas

Focus on one or two phrases, and plant them in your heart and head so you can speak sojourn!

This will also help you keep setting your mind on and seeking things above.

2. Seek Heaven

Read **Hebrews 11:15-16** again. What words describe how the sojourning saints felt, thought, or responded to their "better country"?

The NIV says they were *longing*. The NASB and CSB say they *desired* their true home.

Pause and study your heart. Do you long for and desire your true home in Heaven, your better country? Or are you anchored too solidly in this world? Spend some time thinking and praying. Jot down your thoughts if you want, or just keep it between you and God. Take your time; I'll wait.

Now, review **verse 16**. How did God feel or respond to those heavenly seeking, sojourn-speaking saints?

Oh, this slays me when I really consider it.

God was proud of the Hebrews 11 sojourners who identified with their true country. God is also not ashamed to be called our God when our thoughts and words reflect hearts set on things above.

> The writer of Hebrews could have been inspired to say many things about how God felt about those sojourning saints. Why do you think "unashamed" captured His emotion?

Maybe God was proud of them because He knew what it felt like to be them. We have a sojourning God who came and dwelt among us. He wore our skin. He knows what it feels like to be human, to hurt, grow weary, suffer, and face temptation (Heb. 4:15). But He didn't waver.

> "For the joy set before him he endured the cross, scorning its shame, and sat down at the right hand of the throne of God."

HEBREWS 12:2b

> Write out a sojourn confession and thank God that you do not walk alone. (If you need an example, look at the quote by Tina Boesch at the beginning of this day of study.)

Amen

ACTIONS OF A SOJOURNING SAINT

If we have sojourning speech and a heavenly longing, it should translate into righteous action like it did for Moses.

Read **Hebrews 11:24-26**.

Though Moses had all the privilege of Egypt's palace at his disposal, he didn't grasp it, align himself with it, or exploit it. Instead, he identified with his true country, his true people.

This identification made all the difference in his story.

He discerned between what is fleeting and what is forever, and it dictated his action. Look closely at these verses again to see what I mean.

Hebrews 11:24: What action reflected Moses's sense of identity?

Hebrews 11:25: What was the result of Moses's action?

Hebrews 11:26: What did Moses consider to be his greatest treasure and why?

Moses wasn't just looking at what was right in front of him; he was looking to the reward. It helped him see clearly and act according to his identity.

When we have a sojourn spirit, we're better able to discern between what is temporary and what is permanent. We think and act according to our true identity as citizens of Heaven. We have an eternal perspective.

Read **Hebrews 11:27** to see the result. Either jot down or highlight in your Bible the verbs (action words) in that verse.

A sojourn spirit prompts a willingness to move forward, take risks, and persevere.

Look again at **Hebrews 11:27**. Why did Moses persevere?

I love this! Moses saw Him who was invisible. He had his eye on the One no eye can see. I like how one commentator put it: "Moses paid more attention to the invisible King of kings than to the king of Egypt."[7]

We won't persevere, we won't stay on mission, we won't properly sojourn if we keep our eyes on just what we see. But when we fix our eyes on the One who is the "image of the invisible God," (Col. 1:15) we can finish the race.

> "And let us run with perseverance the race marked out for us, fixing our eyes on Jesus, the pioneer and perfecter of faith."
>
> **HEBREWS 12:1b-2a**

What your faith sees now while you sojourn, your eyes will see when the sojourn ends. Our faith will become sight. The temporary sin we resist, the transient pleasure we forfeit, all will be laughable when we sojourn no more.

Well, that's all. I have no words except about a million *Thank You, Lord*s!

Sojourn well today, my friend. See you tomorrow.

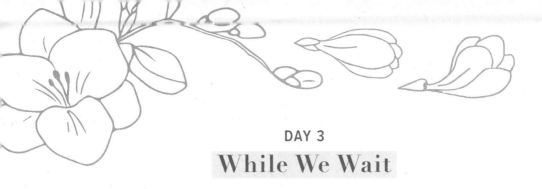

DAY 3
While We Wait

"I must keep alive in myself the desire for my true country,
which I shall not find until after death."[8]

C. S. LEWIS

What activity can you get so involved in that suddenly you notice the clock and say, "Where did the time go?"

I love Fun Friday with my friends. We go to coffee, lunch, shop, have more coffee or Sonic®, shop some more, and then one of us finally says, "It's 5:00 p.m.! Where did the time go?"

I love enjoying something so much I lose track of time!

Well, I loved that feeling until today. Standing at my white glass-top desk, the reality that we only have two more days of study hit me. Where did the time go? I've loved spending these days with you in Heaven, and I will miss it! But even more disappointing to me is this: there is so much more we could learn about Heaven, but we don't have time or pages.

So, since the clock is winding down, let's focus on some passages in Peter's second letter, because he was also running out of time (2 Pet. 1:13-15).

Lord, we want to pay attention to Your Word today, as to a lamp shining in a dark place, until the day dawns and the Morning Star rises in our hearts. Amen (2 Pet. 1:19).

Peter wrote his second letter near the end of his life, expressing concern about false teachers leading the faithful astray. The crux of his message is that we can trust God's Word, count on Christ's return, and keep growing in knowledge and grace so we don't get hoodwinked by naysayers and misleaders (2 Pet. 2:1-3).

> Pour your coffee or tea and read **2 Peter 3** in the CSB or ESV. (Go to biblegateway.com or biblehub.com to find different translations.) Note how many times Peter uses the word *wait* and note what command or comments are associated with the word *wait*.

The word *wait* (waiting) shows up in verses 11-14 in relation to our godliness, holiness, behavior, peacefulness, and posture concerning Christ's return. It's not an impatient waiting but an eager expectation. In fact, the NIV translates the word *look forward*. Peter's words are helping us know what to expect and what to do while we eagerly wait for Christ's return.

WHAT TO DO WHILE WE WAIT

1: Exercise Wisdom

> Read **2 Peter 2:1-3** and **3:3-4**. What is one reason you need wisdom while you wait?

There will be those who come across as slick and believable, who will try to sway you with their stories. Some people will try to make you think you've lost your mind over this idea of Christ's return and a new earth. Skeptics. Mockers. Doubters. False teachers.

> Read Peter's *therefore* in **2 Peter 3:17**. Summarize why you need to be on your guard.

We all need to keep our guard up so we don't fall for lies or fall away.

Let's have the humility to know we can be deceived, distracted, and derailed by all sorts of end times teaching, much of which can tempt us to feel certain about things the Bible is not definitive about.

> *Lord, sanctify us in the truth. Your Word is truth. We trust You with all our hearts. We do not lean on our own understanding. We ask You for wisdom and thank You for giving it to us liberally (John 17:17; Prov. 3:5; James 1:5).*

2: Expect His Return

While we wait for Christ's return, we do so expectantly, because He keeps His promises. But when is He going to return?

> Read **2 Peter 3:8**. How did Peter reply to the scoffers and skeptics who mocked God's timing (vv. 3–4)?

Peter jolted them back into God's time with a reminder that God's ways are not our ways. The skeptics who made fun and the false teachers who were so certain about the timing of Christ's return were operating in the wrong time zone—their own!

We do not know when Jesus will come back; we only know He will (Matt. 24:36).

> But read what **2 Peter 3:9** says about the grace that fills every minute of God's time. If we see His return as taking way too long, why is He allegedly "slow"?

Isn't that just like our Father? He isn't willing that any of us miss out on being with Him forever. If you don't know Him, His grace is extending to you right now, giving you another opportunity to trust and receive Him. And if you do know Him, His grace is extending through you as you tell others how to know Him. As we wait, we are to be about the mission

Christ has called us to in making disciples. As Paul said, we are entrusted with the ministry and message of reconciliation. We are to be ambassadors for Christ, pleading with people to be reconciled to Him (2 Cor. 5:18-20).

> Is the expectation of Christ's return motivating you to be on mission for Him? If so, in what way? If not, how can you change that this week?

The coming redemption of the new creation that will be fully realized in that "better country" should flow through you to impact this time and space, your country, this current creation. Can't you see how radical the reality of Heaven is? Since death is defeated, everywhere you walk and every word you speak as a redeemed child of God should eradicate a little more death and darkness (Matt. 5:14-16; Eph. 5:8-14).

We want to live with that kind of urgency and certainty in light of the ultimate completion.

> We must do so because of what Peter said in **2 Peter 3:10**. How did he describe the day of Christ's return?

We don't know when Jesus will return any more than we know when a bad guy may break into our homes. (But have your Halloween mask ready just in case. Wink.)

Lord, at the right time You will bring everything in Heaven and earth together under the authority of Christ (Eph. 1:10). May we serve You, Your people, all people You love and created and this current creation according to Your redemptive plan and grace in and through us. Amen.

3: Elevate Godly Living

> Read **2 Peter 3:11-12**. Based on Christ's imminent return, what was Peter telling us we should do?

Our lives should be godly and holy.

> But hold that thought for a sec and look at **verse 13**. What does it say our posture concerning the new earth should be?

> At this point in our study, I'm curious. Are you looking forward to that day when you inhabit the new earth? Yes or No? Why?

My mom texts me most days and asks if I "will be in Heaven today." Of course, she means in the Heaven manuscript, not the actual place.

But if I were to go today, I'm okay with that, because I feel far more anchored in the reality of eternity at this point and I'm growing in anticipation of living fully in my glorious unending. I'm not ready to leave here, but I am really looking forward to there.

Let's live here; long for there. Flourish here; yearn for there.

Okay, circling back to verses 11-12, let's build on what Peter said about godly and holy living.

> Look at **verse 14** in the NASB.

> Peter told us that while we wait eagerly for the new heavens and the new earth, what are we to be?

> **Be**

> **Be**

We are to *be* diligent to *be* found spotless and blameless and at peace.

The CSB and NIV use the phrase *make every effort to be found . . . .* The big takeaway here is the phrase *be found.*

> Ponder what it means to "be found."

Think about this. I can't drive. So I can't *be found* at my favorite coffee shop, sipping an extra hot, double shot, breve latte if I was not driven there, right?

Well, apply that to being spotless, blameless, and at peace. You can't be found that way if you aren't made that way to begin with. Just like I can't get myself to a coffee shop to be found there, you can't get yourself to blamelessness, spotlessness, and peacefulness unless the spotless Lamb, the Prince of peace, takes your blame and places you in His righteousness. You are found there because Jesus gets you there.

That is your spiritual position, which means it should also be your practice and pursuit. Yes, Jesus makes you spotless and blameless; so, pursue the life of righteousness Jesus died to give you. Practice what His Word says. Christ does the work, but through His Spirit we get to pursue a life that reflects Him in our words and actions. That is how we live out our identity as His daughters—found in Him.

So be diligent to be found in that position. Trust Him and His saving and redemptive work in you.

Peace with God means we are to be at peace with each other. In this we reflect our citizenship and our King. Jesus is the Prince of peace, and when His subjects, His brothers and sisters, squabble, back bite, or choose dissention, we don't reflect our true country and call. Who in the world would want to inhabit the new earth with us forever if we are fighting, disagreeable, and quick to point out why we're right and everyone else is wrong?

Pause and study your heart.

If you took your last breath today or if Christ returned, would you be found pursuing the life of blamelessness and purity you've been set apart for?

Would He find you at peace with your family, your church, your colleagues, neighbors, your online community?

Do you need to make peace in any relationships in your life? Most importantly, do you need to make peace with God through repentance and belief in Jesus?

If you have broken relationships, it may be hard and humbling to apologize, forgive, overlook, or reconcile, but it is so worth it. Earth is short; Heaven is long.

So, let's be found at peace when it is under our control (Rom. 12:18).

> ". . . continue in him, so that when he appears, we may be confident and unashamed before him at his coming."

1 JOHN 2:28

Lastly, read **2 Peter 3:18**. What was Peter's final instruction, the one that summarizes how all we talked about today is possible?

Grow in _____!

Oh, my friend. Grace, grace, grace. ("Grace, grace, grace" is also one of my Speak Sojourn phrases!)

Paul tells us why we need to grow in grace in **Titus 2:11-13**. Why is grace so important?

It is by grace we are saved. It is grace that teaches us to say no to ungodliness, and it is grace that empowers us to live according to our heavenly citizenship. So may we all keep growing in grace like a blossoming blue flower springing from the fertile soil and green grass of Heaven!

All right, that's enough for now. Tomorrow will be our last day of study, followed by your last *Dash Living Day*. (Insert melancholy sigh.)

I'm lighting my blue flower candle to celebrate you and our glorious unending with the One our souls love. Praise You, Jesus.

Dying Well

"It's in death that God says, 'If I'm not your security, then you've got no security, because I'm the only thing that can't be taken away from you. I will hold you in my everlasting arms. Every other set of arms will fail you, but I will never fail you.'"[9]

TIM KELLER

I'm beginning our time here with a steaming hot cup of coffee and a big, wistful sigh. I've imagined you sitting at my kitchen table or leaning back in my mustard-colored library chair in my office for weeks. We're listening to the crackling of my blue flower candle and enjoying its aroma as I write, thinking and talking through Heaven together. But after today, poof, you're gone! We won't be spending so much time together. It's a good thing we have eternity, right?

Over the last few weeks, we've talked about what it will be like when our faith becomes sight in the present Heaven and on the new earth. And we've also talked about how to live now in light of our heavenly reality. But we haven't talked yet about how to die. And according to the bureau of statistics, there is a one hundred percent chance that's going to happen. Unless, of course, Christ returns first.

I hope by this point you're so convinced your future is bursting with hope that getting honest about dying is not a morbid subject. Grab your favorite drink, and let's finish well.

Thank You, God, that not only each of our lives but also each of our deaths are precious to You. Comfort us if we feel anxious or worried. May Your joy be our consolation. Amen (Ps. 72:14; 94:19; 116:15).

It just so happens that I'm writing this on the anniversary of my Hero Dad's death. It was a day of unbearable grief for me and unspeakable glory for him. Isn't that just the nature of death for believers—a conflicted cocktail of opposites.

Fill in the blank spaces of the chart below to show the opposite realities of death. (I've done the first as an example for you.)

HARD REALITY	HOPEFUL REALITY
Exit	Entrance
End	
	Reunion
Loss	
	Joy

Each opposite reality is absolutely true, and each carries its own emotion. We can't change the realities associated with death, but we can choose how we view it. We can see it only as a hard reality or only as a hopeful one. But neither is healthy or realistic. We need to embrace death as both at the same time—both hard and hopeful.

The defeat comes when we get stuck in the "Hard Reality" column, and all we feel is the sting—separation, loss, and sorrow. That causes us to fear and dread our death and grieve the death of others like those "who have no hope" (1 Thess. 4:13).

Yet, let's be candid and tender with each other about this. Even if we're comforted by the hopeful reality of death, the fear of death is real; that applies to our own and those we love. It always ranks high among people's greatest fears, if they are brave enough to admit it.

Do you fear death? If so, why? Be honest.

I think I fear death because I don't want to suffer or be in pain. I dread the uncertainty of how my life may end, and I worry about leaving my people or my people leaving me.

Feel free to analyze the reasons for my fear. Maybe it will help you understand your own. Is it really death I fear? Or just what surrounds it?

Find Psalm 23:4. What was David's view of death, and why?

David fearlessly walked through the darkest valley because God was with him.

Viewing my fear of death through the lens of **Psalm 23**, I can see that it is not really death I fear but the process and the unknowns of the process. How about you? Jot down your thoughts.

Yet, if you know Christ, what was true for David in Psalm 23 is true for you. You will not encounter death alone. In the uncertainty and shadows is your unseen Shepherd. He will be with you every step of the way as you walk through the shadows, from the valley through the veil and into the "house of the LORD forever" (Ps. 23:6).

My friend, it's okay to feel all the hard realities associated with death, but you do not need to fear it because God will be with you. He will be with your loved ones also.

I know that some of us, perhaps including you, have people we love who have died and we're not certain they knew Jesus as Savior and Lord. First, my heart breaks for you having to carry that grief and uncertainty. But let me give you a possible comforting thought and a challenge. No one knows the heart of a person except God. Your loved one may have had a faith moment even with his or her last breath. It happened like that for a thief (Luke 23:39-43). We just don't know. What I do know is we probably all have friends or family still alive who don't yet know Christ. May we feel the urgency to share the love of Jesus with them.

Part of the way we can reduce our fear of death and die well is to think about how we want to leave this earth. To help us in that, let's note some of the final words of those who died in Scripture.

1: Stephen

Review **Acts 7:56-60**. Stephen's last words were two distinct requests in prayer. What was the first in verse 59?

Like Jesus on the cross, Stephen asked God to receive his spirit. What a beautiful closing remark for his life on this earth. Yet I wonder, what if we let his last words influence our first thoughts?

How would your day be different if you started with similar words? Lord, receive my spirit today. Not in a passing from this life to the next meaning, but in a "take my life, let my whole self be yours" way. What do you think?

We want to give our whole selves to God every day. Ask God to receive your whole self each morning.

> " . . . whoever loses his life for My sake will find it."
>
> ### MATTHEW 16:25b (NASB)

The second thing Stephen prayed before he died was really amazing. What did Stephen ask God to do in verse 60?

Again, like Christ on the cross, Stephen, in a spirit of forgiveness, asked God to forgive those who hurt him. Wow. Perhaps because Stephen didn't hold on to his own life he could also let go of hurt and offenses and forgive.

Stephen's last words were about forgiveness. It makes sense that he couldn't, in good conscience, ask God to forgive his trespassers if that was not also his heart. What if you forgive quicker and let go of hurts and offenses as you give your life wholly to Jesus? If you want to leave with a clear conscience and clean slate, why not start now?

What if you live how you want to leave?

So, is there anyone you need to forgive? Or seek the forgiveness of someone you wronged? Don't wait until your last breath to do it.

If you need to forgive or seek forgiveness, commit that action to the Lord in prayer, then take necessary steps to clear your conscience and your heart.

My Forgiveness Prayer

"Forgive us our debts, as we also have forgiven our debtors."

MATTHEW 6:12

2: Jacob

Read **Hebrews 11:21**. In what two distinct ways/words did Jacob finish his life?

He blessed and worshiped. Living well and dying well can be found in those two simple acts—bless others, worship God.

Remember on the Session Four *Dash Living Day* (p. 137) you shared your blessings. You can live those blessings even now. Ask God to guide you to behave, speak, and serve as a blessing to others. Don't let the only blessings you give be the ones you leave. Let them be the blessings you live. And let's strive to be like Jacob, who in his last days chose to turn his face to God and worship the One who encountered him, led him, and blessed him. May our faces and hearts be turned in the same way, not just in our dying breath but in every breath we take.

"Let the words of my mouth and the meditations of my heart be acceptable in Your sight . . . "

PSALM 19:14 (ESV)

Oh, what a great way to die well and live well all at once.

Your age may be twenty seven, seventy seven, or somewhere in between. (Or maybe you're way past seventy seven! Way to go, wonder woman!) Regardless of how long you've lived, you do not know when you will exhale your last breath here. So why not live ready to die? Why not be a woman who blesses people and worships God every day you live? Why not live as a forgiver? Why not live fully committed, abandoned to Christ in light of Heaven's promise?

Living with focus reduces dying with fear.

We don't know what it feels like to die. We don't know what it is like to close our eyes to this earth and open them in Heaven. But perhaps we can use our imagination and compare it to something we do understand: birth.

A little human grows and develops nestled safely in her mother's womb. She is safe and sheltered. That warm cocoon is her whole world.

Yet her world is so very tiny and dark. Like a fish in an aquarium, it is the only world she knows. Like that fish doesn't know water is wet and has no idea he's surrounded by invisible walls, that tiny baby doesn't know she is confined and crowded with no air and no light.

Her mother marvels at how every kick and elbow is met with boundaries. Each poke and nudge another reminder that the baby's tiny world can hardly contain her.

But the baby? She is content. She can't conceive that her world is not the world. She doesn't know the dark is dark.

Not until it is her time to travel through the birth canal and be born into the world she was created to live in, the world of light and air and boundlessness.

Could that be what it feels like to die?

Here on this side of eternity, we think this world is it. We think we know shelter and freedom and light. But in reality, we only see shadows. We fear death because we really don't know what it feels like to be fully alive.

But there will be a day when we awaken to the true light, to unending boundless freedom and love, to live in the world we were created for, to be with the One who created us for Himself.

My friend, don't shy away from talking about death. Don't avoid those who are dying because you feel awkward. Death feels shattering, emptying, and totally counterintuitive, but death is defeated.

George Herbert wrote, "Death used to be an executioner, but the Gospel makes him just a gardener."[10]

Death used to be able to crush us, but now all death can do is plant us in God's soil so we become something extraordinary.

Death isn't the period at the end of our stories. Death is the comma that transitions us from the prologue to the forever stories of our lives. Death allows you to step fully into your glorious unending, finally trading faith for sight.

I'll write it one last time: earth is short, and Heaven is long.

May we live well and die well all for the glory of God.

And all the sisters said, Amen!

Okay, until our faith becomes sight, onward and upward!

I'm cheering you on. Thanks for spending time with me in Heaven.

I can't wait to see you, yes, I mean truly see you there!

Love,

Jennifer

TAKEAWAY TRUTHS

Below are some important points we covered this week. There's also room for you to add other takeaways you want to remember.

- As believers, we live in the "now, but not yet," having received all the spiritual blessings in Christ but not yet fully received them. We are part of the kingdom of God here and now, but His kingdom will not come to ultimate fulfillment until Christ returns.

- This world isn't our true home, so we shouldn't get too comfortable here. But while we're here, we should have an eternal mindset, letting our destination dictate our purpose and priorities.

- We should be eagerly and expectantly awaiting Christ's return, growing in grace and holiness, and being about the business of the kingdom—making disciples. We should also be focusing on what's most important—loving God and loving others.

- A question that should constantly be on our hearts: if Christ came today, in what spiritual condition would He find me?

- We should live how we want to leave. We should make sure we are keeping short accounts with a heart ready to forgive.

MY DASH LIVING DECLARATIONS

Until that last day, you get to live within the dashes—that time between your birth and your death. So, think about how you want to live out the rest of your days, be they many or few, in light of what you've learned about Heaven.

Use the prompts below to make some Dash Living Declarations.

Lord, I want the theme of my life to be:

Lord, I want to use my talents and gifts to:

Lord, I want to love people well in these ways:

Lord, I want to honor you with my life by:

"For to me, to live is Christ and to die is gain."

PHILIPPIANS 1:21

WALKING BY FAITH UNTIL FAITH BECOMES SIGHT

BEFORE THE VIDEO

Welcome and Prayer

WATCH THE VIDEO

TWO PRINCIPLES FOR WALKING BY FAITH UNTIL FAITH BECOMES SIGHT:

1. **Learn to Wait** _____

   • Women who walk by faith wait on God _____.

   • Women who walk by sight wait for _____ from God.

   • When our faith becomes sight, we'll realize God was worth the _____.

Biblical waiting is an _____ anticipation.

2. _____

   • The woman who walks by faith _____.

   • The woman who walks by sight might have a tendency to _____.

   • When your faith becomes sight, your faithfulness will be _____ as you receive a crown of life.

Get this last teaching summary sent to your inbox by visiting **jenniferrothschild.com/heaven**. You'll also find all sorts of *Heaven* swag to help you keep walking by faith until your faith becomes sight.

To access the video teaching sessions, use the instructions in the back of your Bible study book.

CONVERSATION GUIDE

PERSONAL BIBLE STUDY

- What was your favorite day of study? Why?

- Explain the concept of living in the "already" and the "not yet"? How should this reality shape our existence, our purpose, our focus?

- What does it mean for us to continually seek things above and set our minds on things above? Why is it important and how do we do it?

- Are you currently living with a sojourn spirit? If so, what's the evidence? If not, what's holding you back?

- If Christ returned today, would He find you waiting well—chasing the right pursuits, faithfully stewarding relationships, living on mission? Explain.

- What are your honest thoughts about death? How has this study affected the way you think about it?

- Which *Takeaway Truth* stands out to you and why?

- *Dash Living Day*: Share some of your Dash Living Declarations.

VIDEO TEACHING

- What's one thing that stood out to you from the video teaching? Why?

- How would you define biblical waiting? Why is it important that we embrace the posture of biblical waiting?

- What's the difference in waiting on God alone and waiting on the things of God? What is your tendency to do and why?

- What does it mean to persevere and not shrink back as believers?

- As you persevere, are you able to delight in all things? Even the hard things? Explain.

Leader Helps

Thanks so much for leading your group through this study! I know you'll experience joy and lots of blessings as you walk your group through the study of Heaven. I'm praying for you as you take on this responsibility.

Find leader resources at **lifeway.com/heaven**. I've also put together lots of good stuff for you at **jenniferrothschild.com/heaven**. You'll find extra resources, links to imaginative giveaways for your group members, and samples of the most creative ways leaders are making this study fun and meaningful. And you can share your ideas there too.

STUDY FORMAT

GROUP SESSIONS: Each group session contains the following elements: Welcome and Prayer / Watch the Video / Conversation Guide. You can access the video content from the card in the back of your Bible study book. The conversation guide provides questions generated from the previous week of personal study and the video teaching. Feel free to adapt, skip, or add questions according to the needs of your group.

PERSONAL STUDY: Each session contains four days of personal study and finishes with a *Dash Living Day* to help women reflect on how they are presently living their lives and the legacy they leave behind. Each week of study also includes a *Takeaway Truths* page that provides several summary statements that emphasize and clarify important points studied during the week.

BEING AN EFFECTIVE LEADER

Three keys to being an effective leader of your group:

1. **PREPARE.** Watch the teaching videos and complete each week of personal study before the group session. Review the conversation guide and consider ones to highlight to lead your group through this time.

2. **PRAY.** Set aside time each week to pray for yourself and each member of your group. Though organizing and planning are important, protect your time of prayer before each gathering.

3. **CONNECT.** Find ways to interact and stay engaged with the women in your group throughout the study. Make use of social media, emails, and handwritten notes to encourage them. Urge your group members to connect with each other through the same channels. And don't stop the connection when the study ends. Continue to encourage and challenge the women in your group in their spiritual journeys.

Bible Study Resources

There are so many resources available to help us dig deeper into God's Word. It's wonderful, but it can be overwhelming. Where to start? Who to trust? Here are a few tried and true go-to resources you can use during this study and beyond.

ONLINE TOOLS

- biblehub.com

- biblegateway.com

- biblestudytools.com

- blueletterbible.org

- The *Bible* app (YouVersion)

- *Dwell* audio Bible app (Visit **jenniferrothschild.com/dwell** to see me use it and hear why it's one of my favorites.)

- gotquestions.org

- Logos Bible Software (logos.com)

STUDY TOOLS & BOOKS

- *The New Strong's Expanded Exhaustive Concordance of the Bible* by James Strong

- *Matthew Henry's Concise Commentary on the Whole Bible*

- *Holman Bible Commentaries*

- *The New American Commentaries*

- *The Zondervan Encyclopedia of the Bible* by Merrill C. Tenney and Moisés Silva

- *Heaven* by Randy Alcorn

- *Ultimate Guide to Heaven and Hell* by E. Ray Clendenen

- *Surprised by Hope* by N. T. Wright

- *He Descended to the Dead* by Matthew Y. Emerson

ENDNOTES

Introduction

1. C. S. Lewis, *The Last Battle* (New York, NY: HarperCollins, 1994), 213.

Session One

1. Elizabeth Barrett Browning, *Aurora Leigh* (London: Chapman and Hall, 1857), 304.
2. Britannica, T. Editors of Encyclopaedia, "the blue flower," Encyclopedia Britannica, August 11, 2009, https://www.britannica.com/art/the-blue-flower-literature.
3. C. S. Lewis, *Surprised by Joy: The Shape of My Early Life* (Harcourt, Inc., 1955).
4. Strong's G3614: oikia, Blue Letter Bible, https://www.blueletterbible.org/lexicon/g3614/niv/mgnt/0-1/.
5. Jeremiah Burroughs, *The Rare Jewel of Christian Contentment* (London: Peter Cole, 1648), 67.
6. Charles H. Spurgeon, *The Treasury of David: Psalms 73-150* (Peabody, MA: Hendrickson Publishers, 1870).
7. Randy Alcorn, *Heaven* (Carol Stream, IL: Tyndale House Publishers, 2004).
8. Anonymous, "I Can't Feel at Home Any More," 1919.
9. Randy Alcorn, *Heaven* (Carol Stream, IL: Tyndale House Publishers, 2004), 154.

Session Two

1. Alexander McLaren, *The Books of Esther, Job, Proverbs, and Ecclesiastes* (London: Hodder and Stoughton), 347.
2. C. S. Lewis, *The Great Divorce* (New York: Macmillan, 1946), 72.
3. Walter A. Elwell, Entry for 'Hades,' Evangelical Dictionary of Biblical Theology. https://www.studylight.org/dictionaries/eng/bed/h/hades.html. 1996.
4. Strong's G1067: geenna, Blue Letter Bible, https://www.blueletterbible.org/lexicon/g1067/niv/tr/0-1/.
5. Ibid.

6. John Calvin, *Golden Booklet of the True Christian Life* (Grand Rapids, MI: Baker Book House, 1952), 17.
7. C. S. Lewis, *The Great Divorce* (New York: Macmillan, 1946).
8. Rachel Field, *All This and Heaven Too* (New York: The Macmillan Company, 1939) 4, https://archive.org/details/in.ernet.dli.2015.260482/page/n3/mode/2up.
9. John MacArthur and Richard Mayhue, eds., *Biblical Doctrine: A Systematic Summary of Bible Truth* (Wheaton, IL: Crossway, 2017), 323–324.
10. Philip Edgcumbe Hughes, *Paul's Second Epistle to the Corinthians, The New International Commentary on the Old and New Testament* (Grand Rapids, MI: Wm. B. Eerdmans Publishing Co., 1962), 182.
11. Justin Taylor, "What Are the "Rewards" in Heaven and Should They Motivate Us?" The Gospel Coalition, July 18, 2011, thegospelcoalition.org/blogs/justin-taylor/what-are-the-rewards-in-heaven-and-should-they-motivate-us/.

Session Three

1. C. S. Lewis, *Miracles* (New York: Macmillan, 1947).
2. Mark Taylor, *1 Corinthians*, ed. E. Ray Clendenen, vol. 28, *The New American Commentary* (Nashville, TN: B&H Publishing Group, 2014), 371.
3. David Guzik, "1 Corinthians – The Resurrection of Jesus and Our Resurrection," Enduring Word Commentary, https://enduringword.com/bible-commentary/1-corinthians-15/.
4. Martin Luther, quoted in "1 Corinthians – The Resurrection of Jesus and Our Resurrection," Enduring Word Commentary, https://enduringword.com/bible-commentary/1-corinthians-15/.
5. C. S. Lewis, *Miracles* (New York: Macmillan, 1947).
6. Mark Taylor, *1 Corinthians*, ed. E. Ray Clendenen, vol. 28, *The New American Commentary* (Nashville, TN: B&H Publishing Group, 2014), 385.
7. C. H. Spurgeon, Gleanings Among the Sheaves (New York: Sheldon and Company, 1869), 113.

8. Strong's G2334: theōreō, Blue Letter Bible, https://www.blueletterbible.org/lexicon/g2334/csb/tr/0-1/.

9. C. S. Lewis, *Miracles* (New York: Macmillan, 1947).

Session Four

1. Charles R. Swindoll, *Growing Deep in the Christian Life: Essential Truths for Becoming Strong in the Faith* (Grand Rapids, MI: Zondervan, 1986).

2. Randy Alcorn, *Heaven* (Carol Stream, IL: Tyndale House Publishers, 2004).

3. Christy Thornton, theological review of the *Heaven* Bible study

4. Charles Spurgeon, *The Metropolitan Tabernacle Pulpit Sermons, vol. 30* (London: Passmore & Alabaster, 1884).

5. Thomas Moore, Come, Ye Disconsolate, 1816.

6. George MacDonald, George MacDonald: *An Anthology*, Eds. C.S. Lewis, (New York: Penguin Books, 2001).

Session Five

1. C. S. Lewis, *The Last Battle*, (London: The Bodley Head, 1956).

2. Henry Ward Beecher, Thomas W. Handford, Beecher: Christian Philosopher, Pulpit Orator, Patriot, and Philanthropist (Belford, Clarke, & Co., 1887) 75.

3. "Interview with Billy Graham," Christianity Today, accessed June 26, 2024, https://www.christianitytoday.com/ct/2011/januaryweb-only/qabillygraham.html.

4. Nancy Guthrie, "Heaven Will Be Better Than Eden," desiring God, September 1, 2018, https://www.desiringgod.org/articles/heaven-will-be-better-than-eden.

5. Joni Eareckson Tada, *Spontaneous Compassion* (Grand Rapids, MI: Zondervan, 1997).

6. Richard J. Mouw, *When the Kings Come Marching In* (Grand Rapids: Wm. B. Eerdmans Publishing Co., 2002).

Session Six

1. *The Valley of Vision*, ed. Arthur Bennett (Carlisle, PA: Banner of Truth, 1975), 301.

2. G2212: zēteō, Blue Letter Bible, https://www.blueletterbible.org/lexicon/g2212/kjv/tr/0-1/.

3. Max Anders, *Galatians-Colossians, vol. 8, Holman New Testament Commentary* (Nashville, TN: Broadman & Holman Publishers, 1999), 328.

4. Strong's G5426: phroneō, Blue Letter Bible, https://www.blueletterbible.org/lexicon/g5426/kjv/tr/0-1/.

5. Tina Boesch, *Given: The Forgotten Meaning and Practice of Blessing* (Downers Grove, IL: InterVarsity Press, 2019).

6. Crowder, "Milk & Honey," Milk & Honey album, June 11, 2021, sixsteps Records / Sparrow Records / Capitol CMG.

7. F. F. Bruce, *The Epistle to the Hebrews, Rev. ed., The New International Commentary on the New Testament* (Grand Rapids, MI: Wm. B. Eerdmans Publishing Co., 1990), 314.

8. C. S. Lewis, *Letters to Malcolm: Chiefly on Prayer* (San Diego: Harvest Books, 1992).

9. Timothy Keller, *On Death* (New York, NY: Penguin Random House, 2020).

10. Ibid.

Notes

Notes

Notes

Notes

Notes

Notes

LET'S BE FRIENDS!

BLOG

We're here to help you grow in your faith, develop as a leader, and find encouragement as you go.

lifewaywomen.com

SOCIAL

Find inspiration in the in-between moments of life.

@lifeywomen

NEWSLETTER

Be the first to hear about new studies, events, giveaways, and more by signing up.

lifeway.com/womensnews

APP

Download the Lifeway Women app for Bible study plans, online study groups, a prayer wall, and more!

 Google Play   App Store

Lifeway women

Additional Studies from
JENNIFER ROTHSCHILD

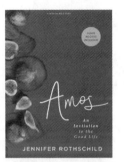

AMOS
8 Sessions

Learn about the prophet Amos to discover what true prosperity is.

lifeway.com/amos

ME, MYSELF & LIES
7 Sessions

Examine your thoughts and words to identify the negativity in your daily inner dialogue and replace negative thoughts with positive truths from God's Word.

lifeway.com/memyselfandlies

TAKE COURAGE
7 Sessions

Study the minor prophet of Haggai to learn to see beyond your current circumstances to a future in Christ.

lifeway.com/takecourage

PSALM 23
7 Sessions

Explore the depths of God's compassionate care while gaining fresh insight and encouragement from Psalm 23.

lifeway.com/psalm23

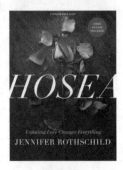

HOSEA
7 Sessions

Dive into the passionate love story of Hosea to identify the modern-day idols in your life and step into the freedom of Christ.

lifeway.com/hosea

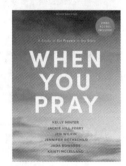

WHEN YOU PRAY
7 Sessions

Join six beloved Bible teachers to study prayers in the Bible that can inspire your own.

lifeway.com/whenyoupray

MISSING PIECES
7 Sessions

Explore the messy, mysterious uncertainties of faith to learn to trust God more.

lifeway.com/missingpieces

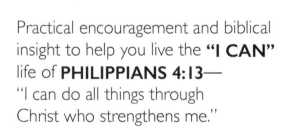

Get the most from your study.

IN THIS STUDY, YOU'LL:

- Dispel the myths and media-influenced images of Heaven to gain a biblical understanding of this essential truth.

- Discover answers to some of your deepest and most pressing questions about Heaven.

- Refine your eternal perspective so you can see beyond this day, this problem, and this situation.

- Realize how your hope for tomorrow should shape how you live today.

STUDYING ON YOUR OWN?

Watch Jennifer Rothschild's teaching sessions, available via redemption code for individual video-streaming access, printed in this Bible study book.

LEADING A GROUP?

Each group member will need a *Heaven* Bible study book, which includes video access. Because all participants will have access to the video content, you can choose to watch the videos outside of your group meeting if desired. Or if you're watching together and someone misses a group meeting, they'll have the flexibility to catch up! A DVD set is also available to purchase separately if desired.

Browse study formats, a free leader guide, a free session sample, video clips, church promotional materials, and more at

lifeway.com/heaven

HERE'S YOUR VIDEO ACCESS.

To stream *Heaven* Bible study video teaching sessions, follow these steps:

1. Go to my.lifeway.com/redeem and register or log in to your Lifeway account.

2. Enter this redemption code to gain access to your individual-use video license:

8CGND37FDLPT

Once you've entered your personal redemption code, you can stream the video teaching sessions any time from your Digital Media page on my.lifeway.com or watch them via the Lifeway On Demand app on any TV or mobile device via your Lifeway account.

There's no need to enter your code more than once! To watch your streaming videos, just log in to your Lifeway account at my.lifeway.com or watch using the Lifeway On Demand app.

QUESTIONS? WE HAVE ANSWERS!
Visit support.lifeway.com and search "Video Redemption Code" or call our Tech Support Team at 866.627.8553.